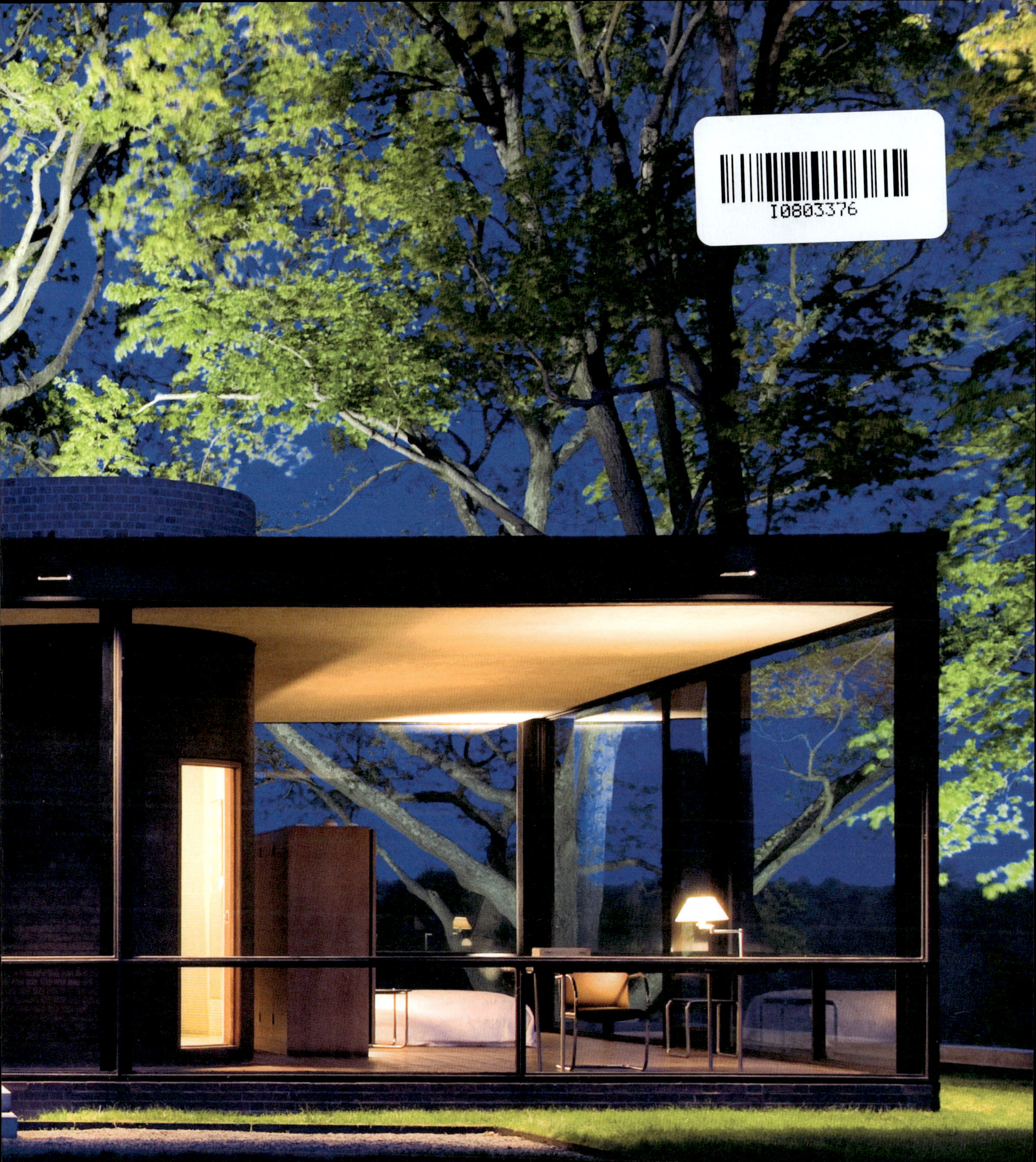

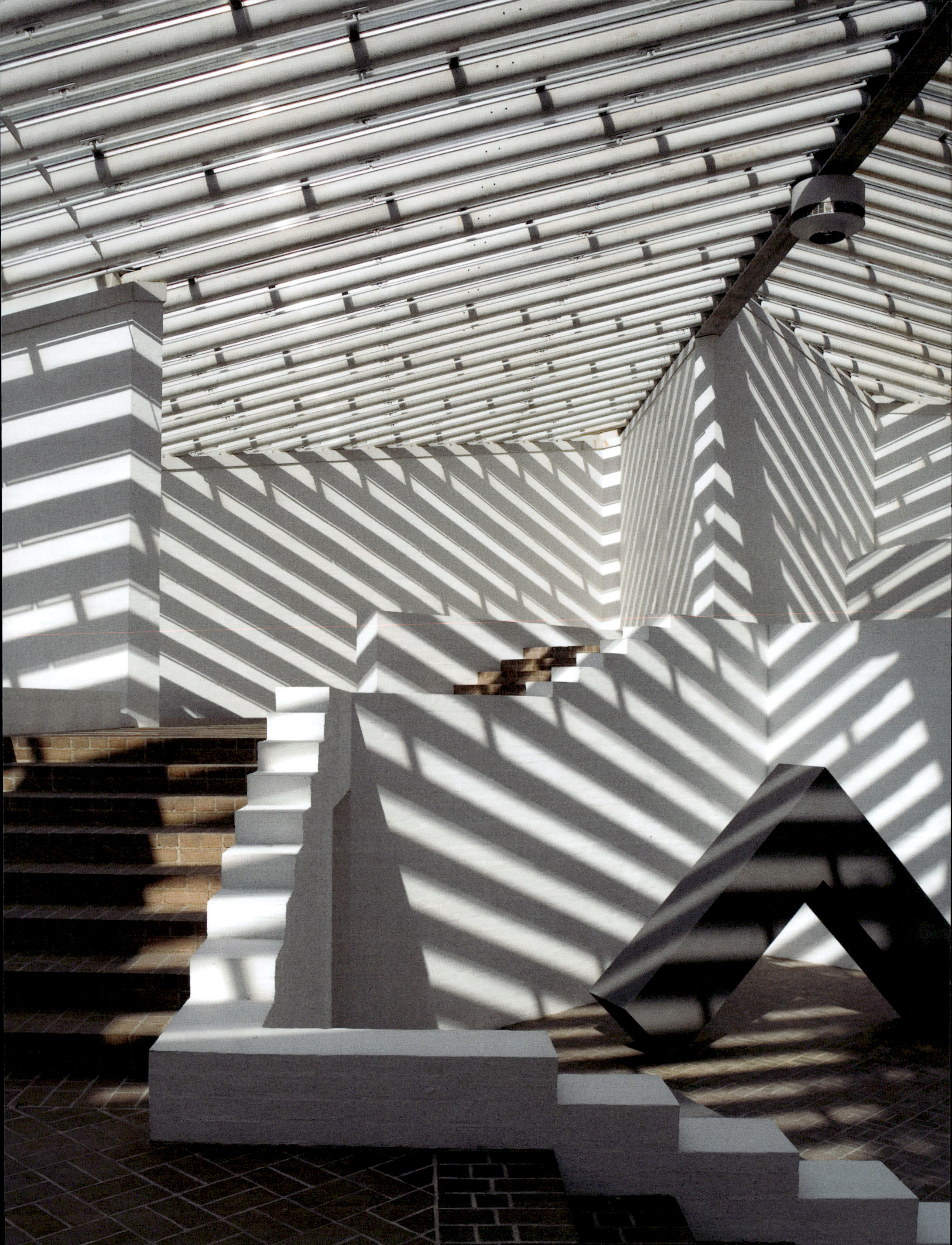

THE GLASS HOUSE COLORING BOOK

COVER ART BY VIK MUNIZ

DRAWINGS BY DAVID WALLACE CROTTY

FOREWORD BY PAUL GOLDBERGER

PROJECT PRODUCED BY SCOTT DREVNIG

POINTED LEAF PRESS

FOREWORD BY PAUL GOLDBERGER

The Glass House is Philip Johnson's autobiography, written in buildings instead of words. It is not a single building but a collection of them, constructed over a span of more than 45 years, during which time Johnson, whose career as an architect was never built on consistency, went from Ludwig Mies van der Rohe's greatest acolyte to an apostle of classicism in modern architecture, and from there to what came to be called deconstructivism, with plenty of detours in between. Johnson never lost his ability to be excited by architecture and art and to seek out the new. He was like a sponge; whatever he saw that moved him he would try to integrate, somehow, into his own work. And so it was that after he purchased five acres of land in New Canaan, Connecticut, in 1945, to give himself a weekend escape from New York City, he started by building a 55-foot-long box of glass that paid homage to Mies, whom he then considered his master. But the Glass House was no copy: His design both honored and subverted Mies' extraordinary Edith Farnsworth House in Plano, Illinois, a house of glass that had been designed but not yet built at the time Johnson started to build in New Canaan. Mies may have conceived of the notion of a house built largely of glass, but Johnson got his done first, and it was very much his own: symmetrical, with a door in dead center, its structure a dark metal frame finished in black rather than white, the whole thing set down on the earth rather than appearing to float above it, as Mies' house does. And then Johnson gave his glass house a companion, the Brick House, a guest house as solid and closed as the Glass House was transparent. It was already beginning to feel like a compound, not a single building, Miesian and anti-Miesian at the same time, the Glass House using the lightest of materials to build what feels, when you see it, like a structure as heavy and solid as a classical temple.

And from there Johnson was off to the races, next going on to create a pavilion that, like many of his buildings from the early 1960s, uses classically inspired colonnades to try to make an architecture both decorative and modern. After that came a remarkable underground art gallery that invokes sources as disparate as the Greek Treasury of Atreus' tomb and the work of the great English architect, Sir John Soane; and then a sculpture gallery in white that makes you think of the white buildings of the Greek islands; and then a stucco studio with a conical dome; and then a whole other building of torqued, bended forms inspired by the work of the artist Frank Stella. Along the way, as the celebration of architecture seemed to keep ratcheting upwards, so did the connection to landscape, since Johnson and his partner, David Whitney, continued to expand the property, which ultimately came to 49 acres. Without landscape, the notion of a house of glass would have had no meaning at all; when a house is all windows, you must have something to be looking at, and the land, and the views, become everything. The land is the wallpaper, and it changes constantly, not just season to season but also from day to day, hour to hour, minute to minute.

How, then, do you color such a thing? The easy way is to make lots of green and let the house just be there, a neutral presence. Not the least of the wonderful moments the Glass House offers is that when you look toward it, you not only see into it, but all the way through it, to the grass and trees on the other side. But the reality is that the Glass House itself never truly disappears, and it barely even recedes. It only plays at being neutral. It is a foreground building, not a background one. And it is a place of deep, subtle tones, rich in its connections to the earth, a man-made object filled with other man-made objects, full of color, as are all the other structures on this remarkable property. For years now, artists and photographers have used the Glass House as the inspiration for works of art that interpret it, play with it, dance with it—doing things with it that help us see Johnson's original building and all its progeny in new and magical ways. Now, with this new coloring book, everyone can do the same and make the Glass House a canvas of their own.

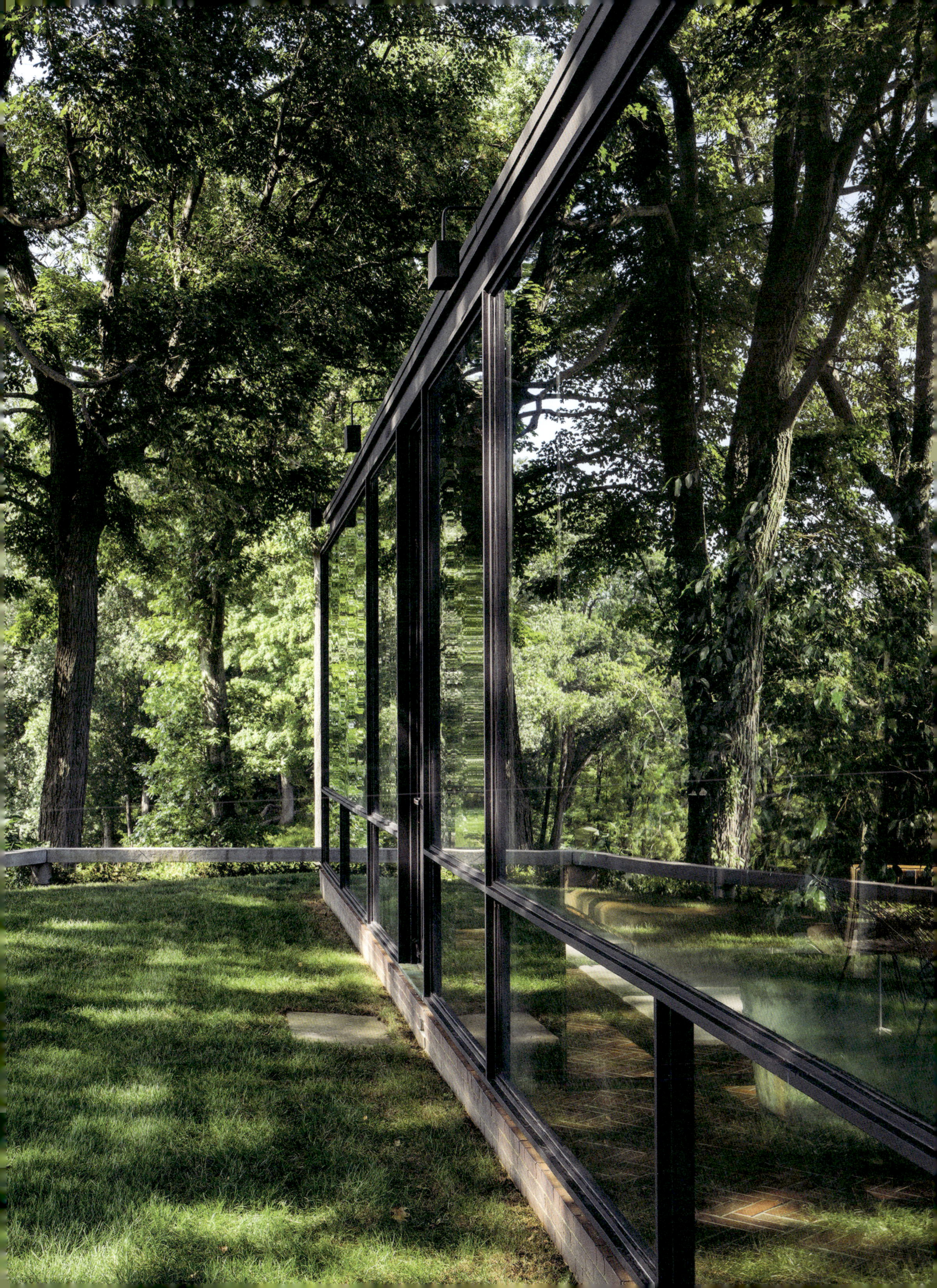

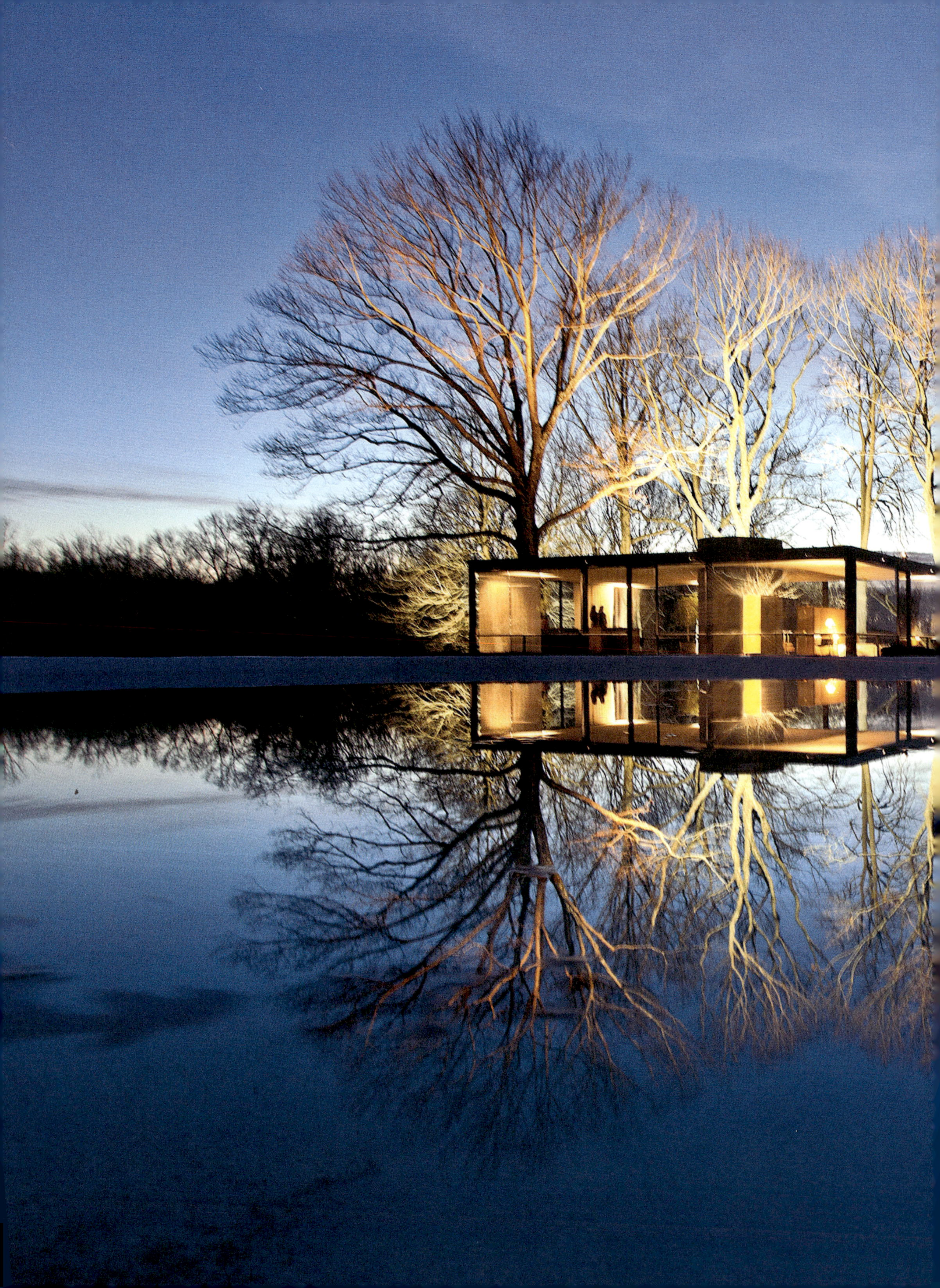

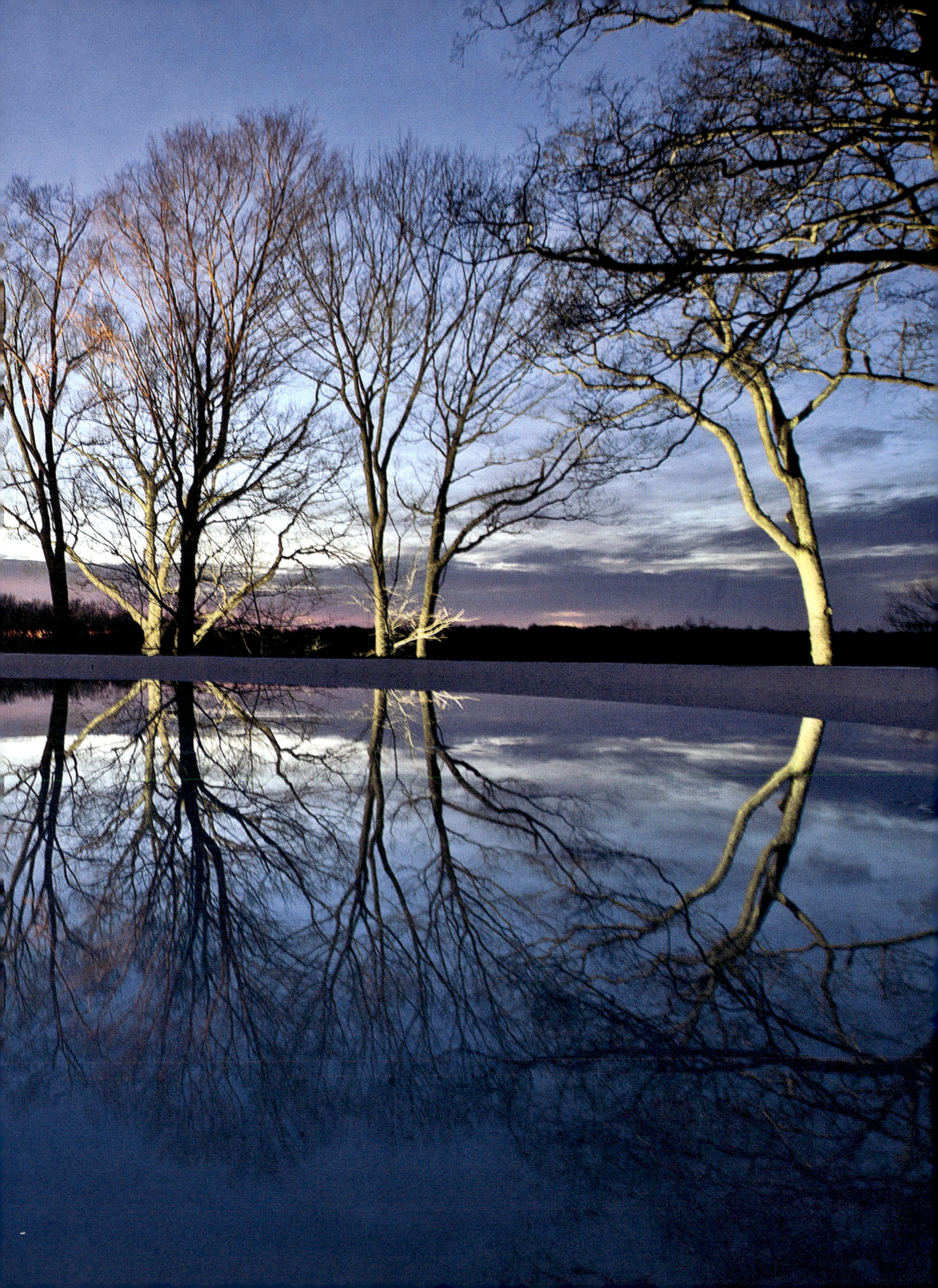

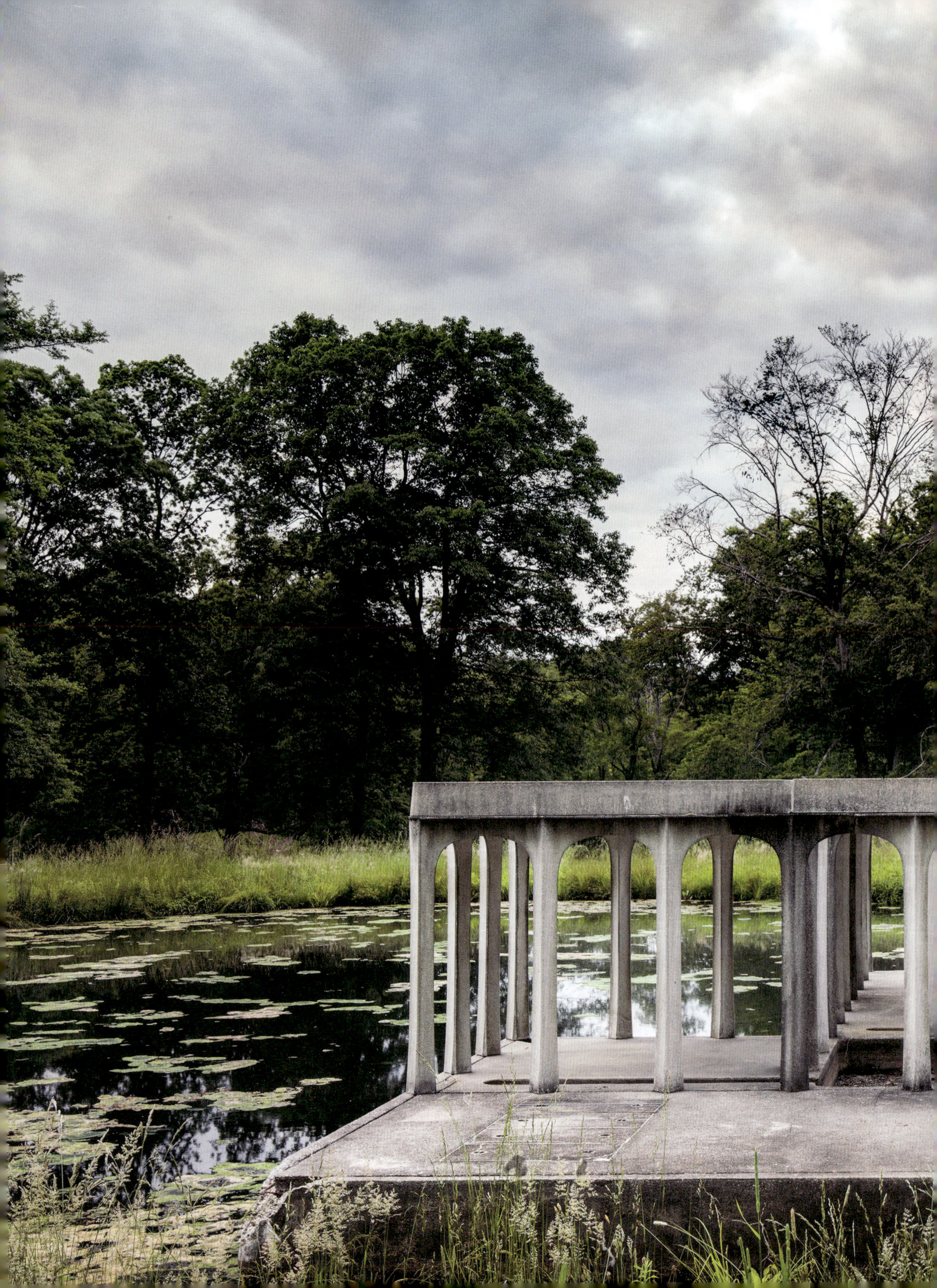

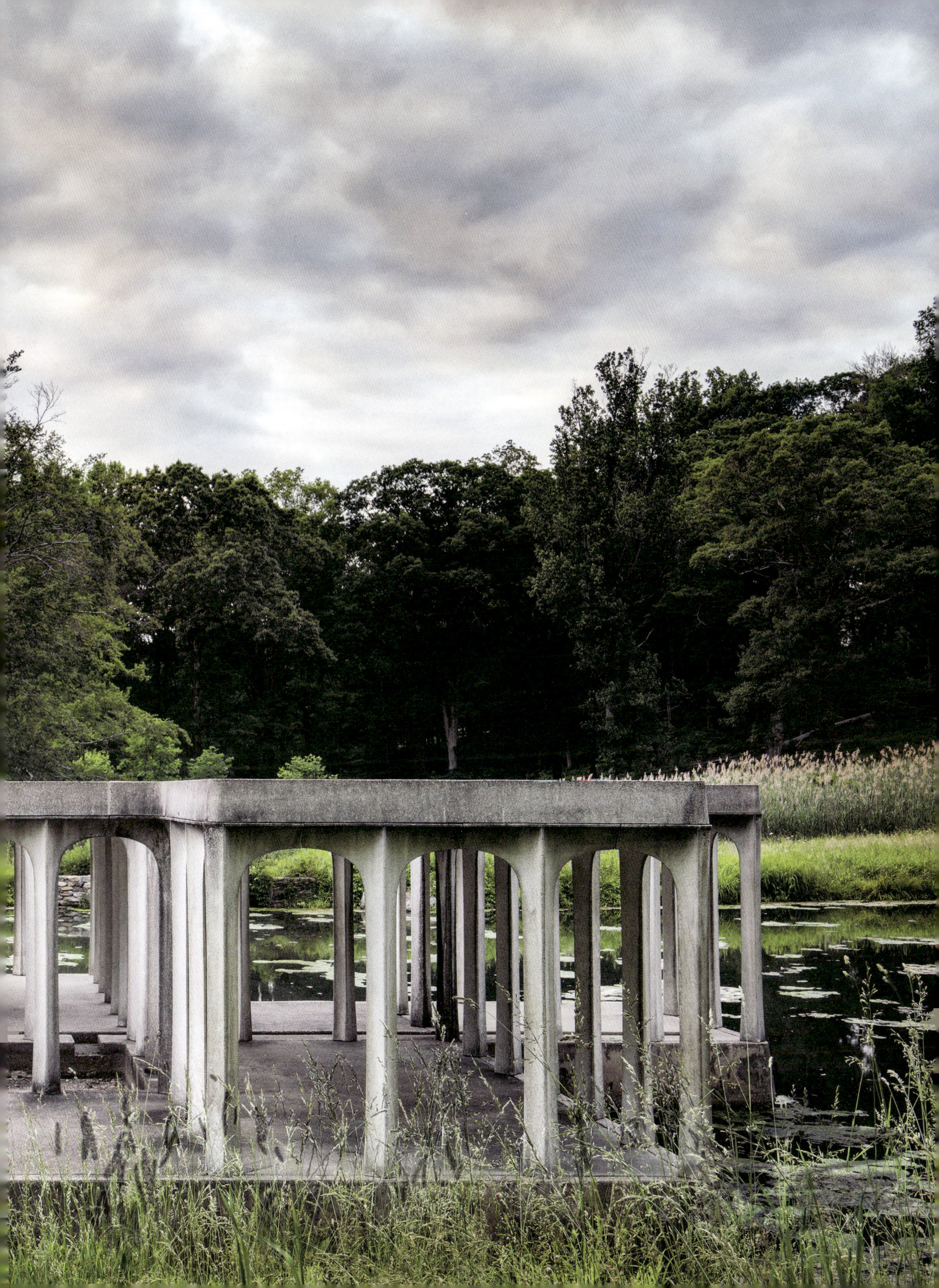

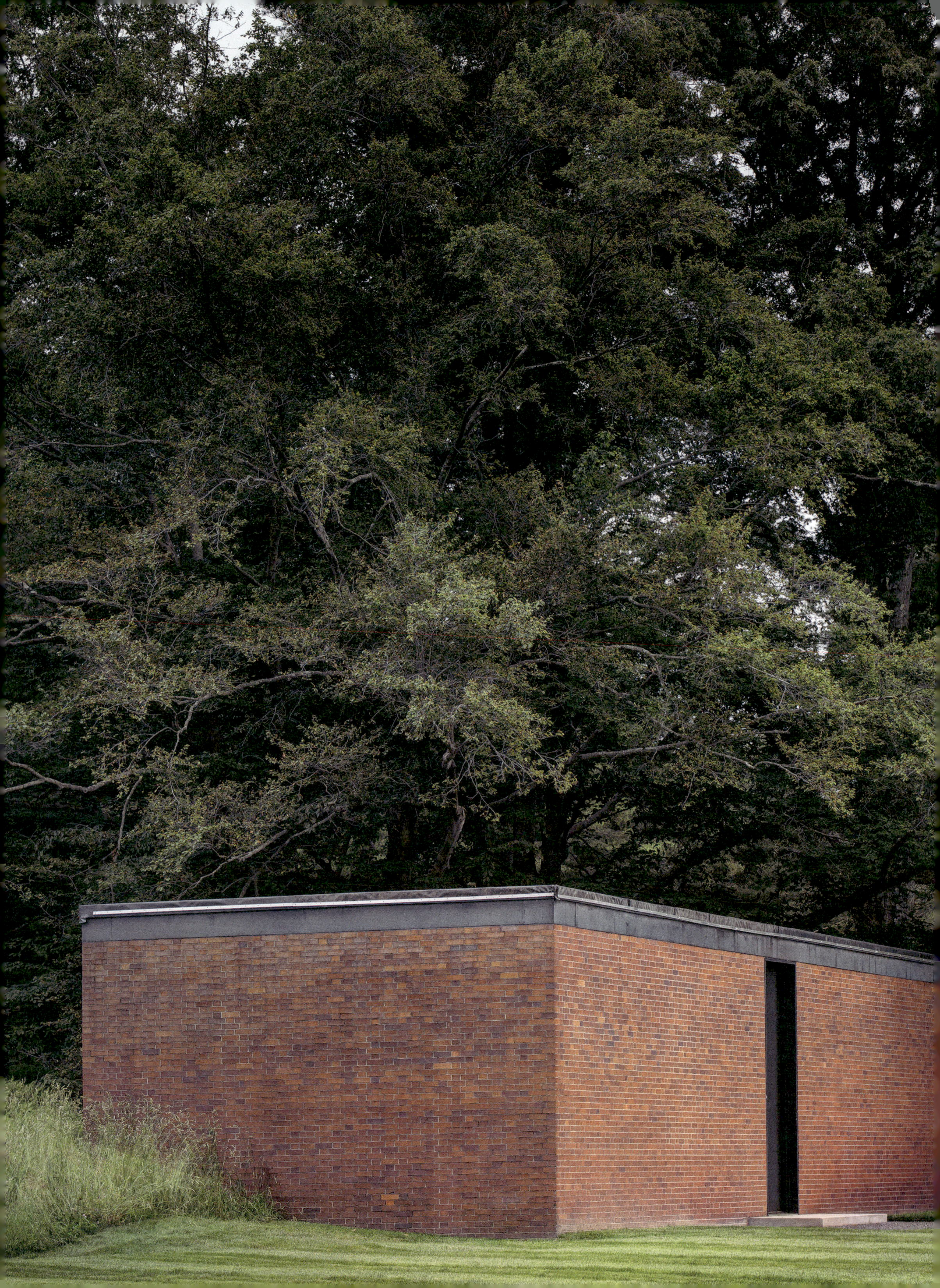

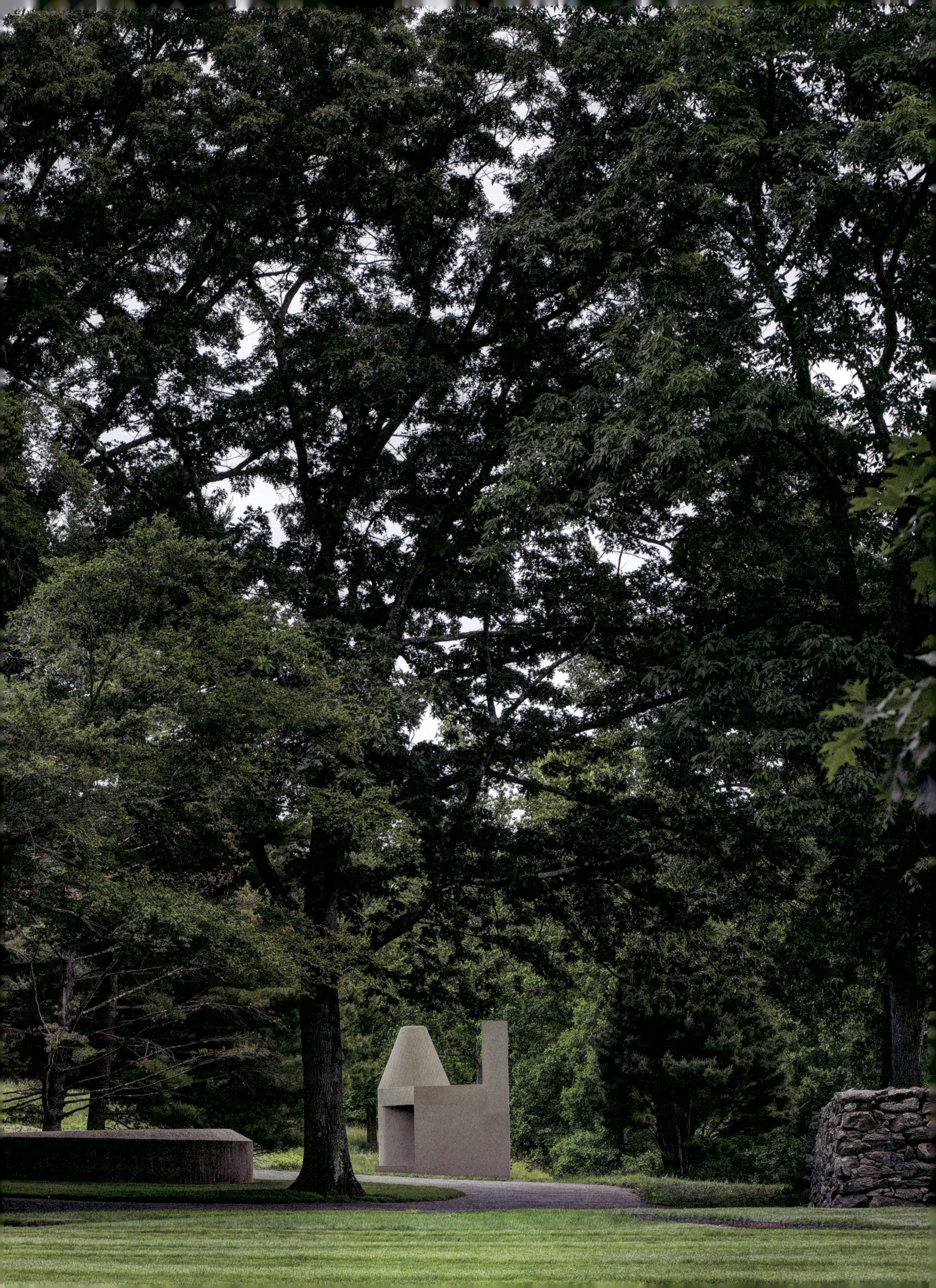

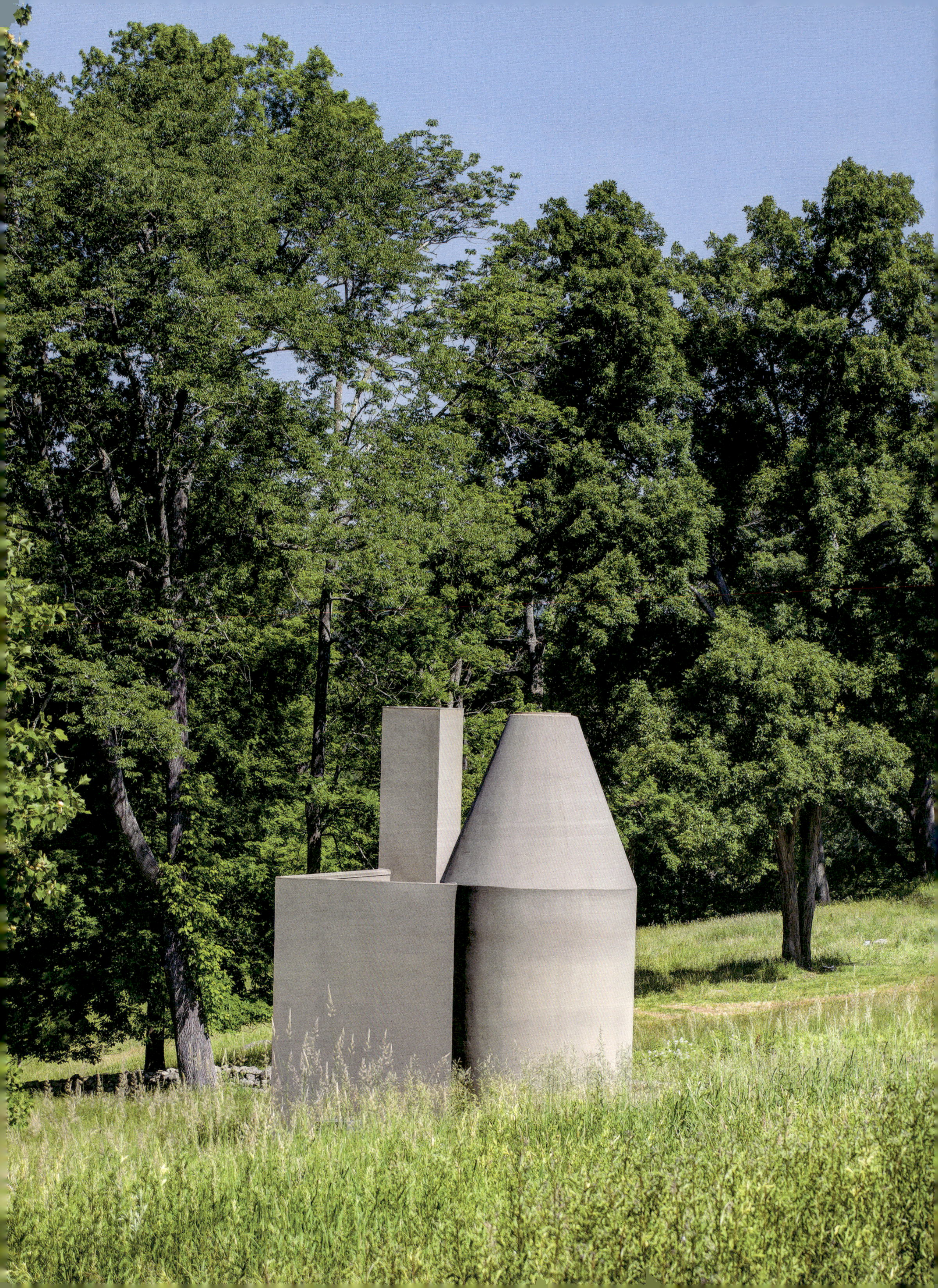

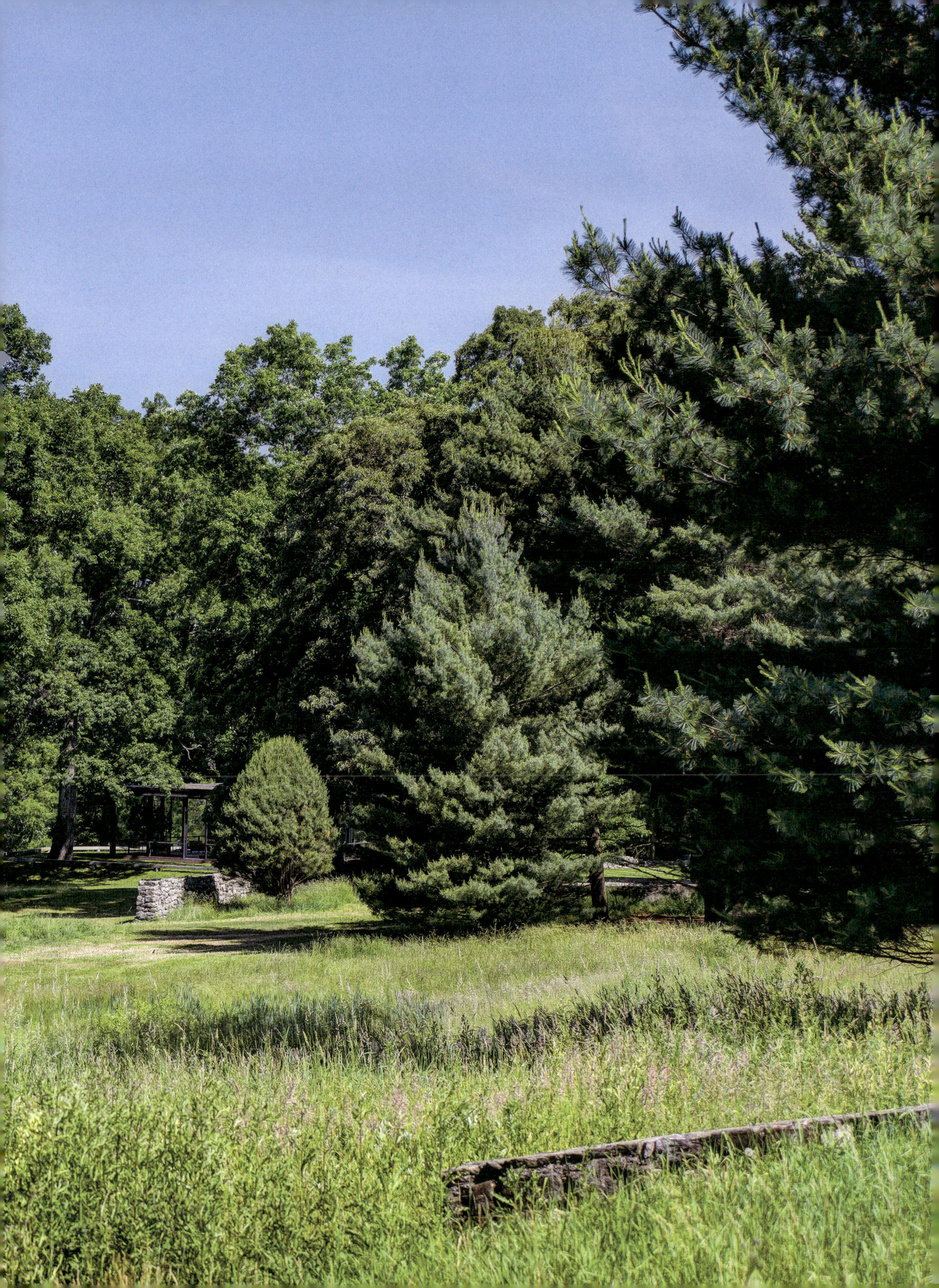

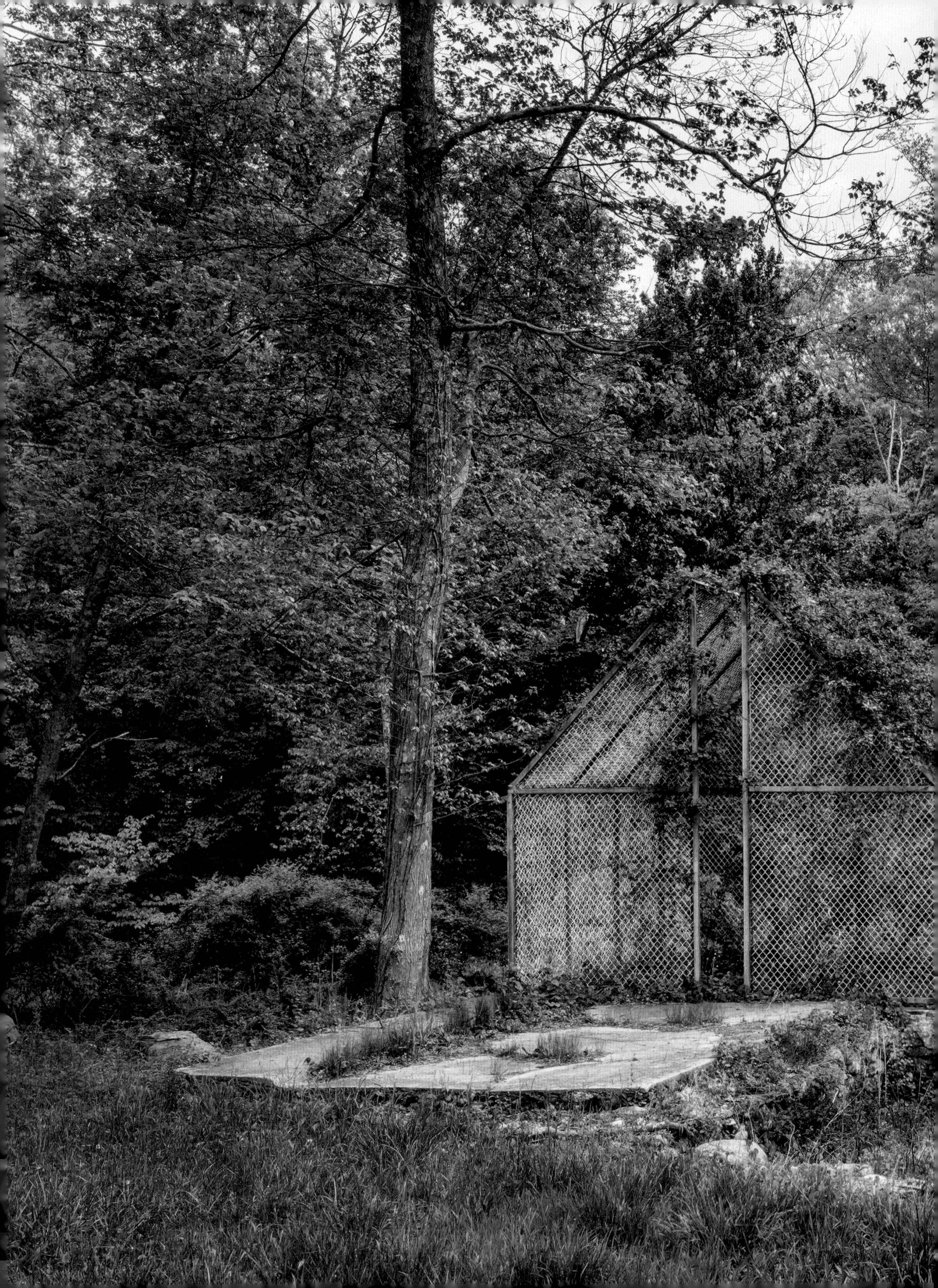

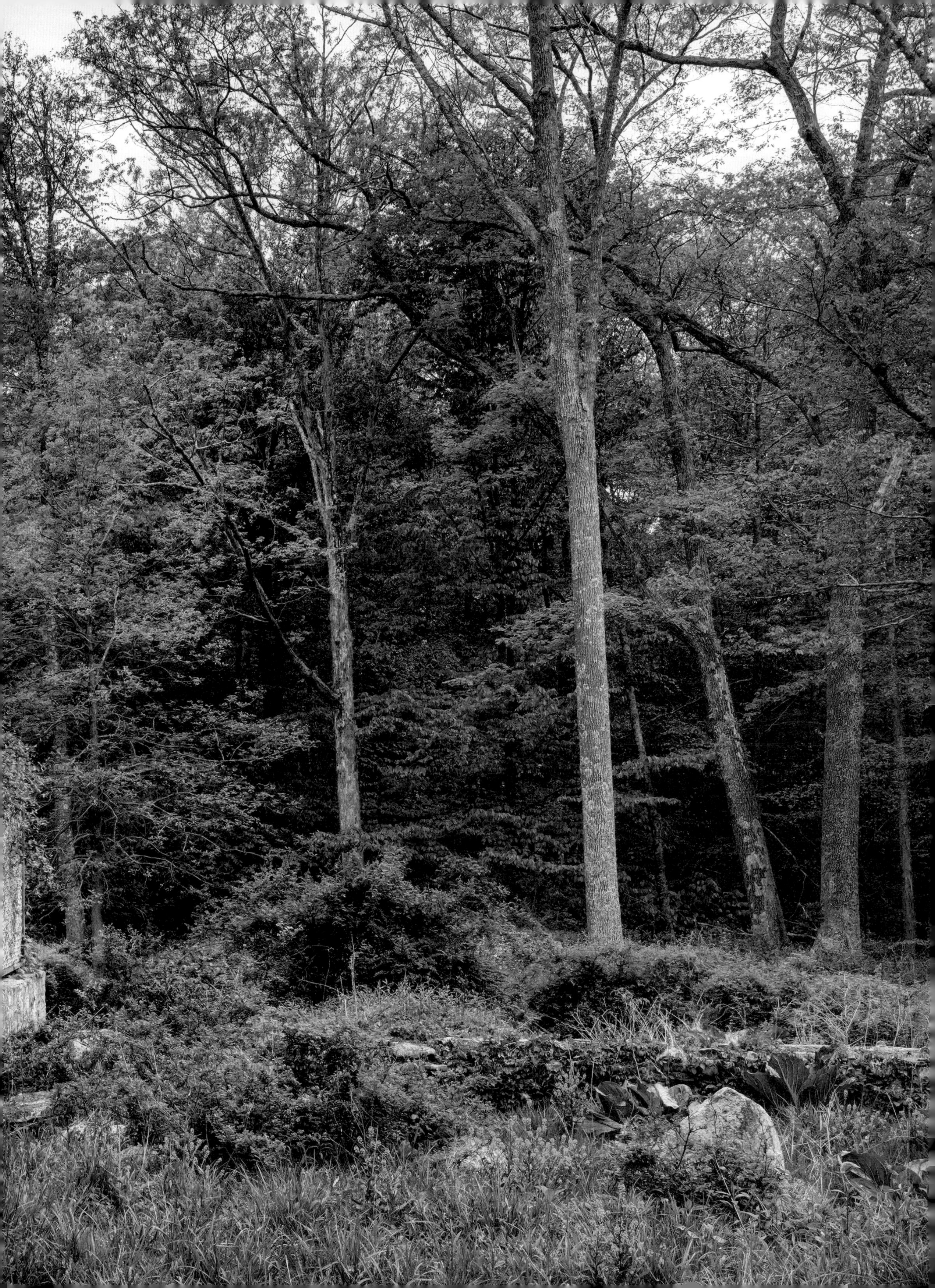

A CAMPUS OF COLOR BY SCOTT DREVNIG

Create beautiful things. That's all. —Philip Johnson

When I was initially offered a position nearly a decade ago at the Glass House, I was thrilled. Although I never had the opportunity to meet its architect, Philip Johnson, in person, I was fully aware of his towering reputation. Johnson had designed some of America's greatest modern architectural landmarks, but the Glass House is his crowning achievement. Situated on 49 acres in New Canaan, Connecticut, and comprised of 14 structures, the site is a masterpiece of modernism and design.

What I was not fully aware of until I began my work at the Glass House was the overwhelming and ever-changing beauty of the place. It was one thing to study the architecture in books and read about the development of the grounds. It was quite another experience to have the opportunity to wander the premises at different times of the year, noticing how the lush plantings, majestic follies, waterfalls, wild turkeys, the deer and the hawks, along with the shifting light and seasons, create an ongoing and ever-surprising landscape. Every day is completely different.

At the Glass House, we've hosted small, one-piece art installations, blockbuster exhibitions, dinners for four guests, parties for 400, intimate concerts, acclaimed dance troupes, a tightrope walker, celebrities posing for magazine covers, private visits for dignitaries, large groups of school children of all ages, fashion photography shoots, historical figures, members of royal families, architecture fans, and much more. Our dedicated team works to preserve our iconic site for future generations, ensuring that there is and will always be a lot to take in and experience.

It has been a pleasure to greet visitors from all over the world who make the journey to our complex off a quiet country road. Some are coming specifically to visit the famed Glass House and are surprised at seeing all of the other buildings, sculptures, and grounds. The transparency of the house ensures that the surrounding natural beauty is visible from inside and out. Like all artists, Johnson has given us an opportunity to see and experience more: More life, more color, more beauty. It is impossible to separate the buildings from the landscape and the light. The combination of all these things creates the magic of the Glass House. A coloring book seems particularly apt, since our site in its entirety is a composition. The colors interact with their surroundings and change from moment to moment.

The aim of this book is to bring the Glass House to you wherever you may be, while honoring the legacy of one of modern architecture's most famous treasures. Whether you have had the opportunity to visit the Glass House or would like to use this book as a way to dream, we welcome you to unleash your vision and create beautiful things with us.

1. THE ENTRANCE GATE

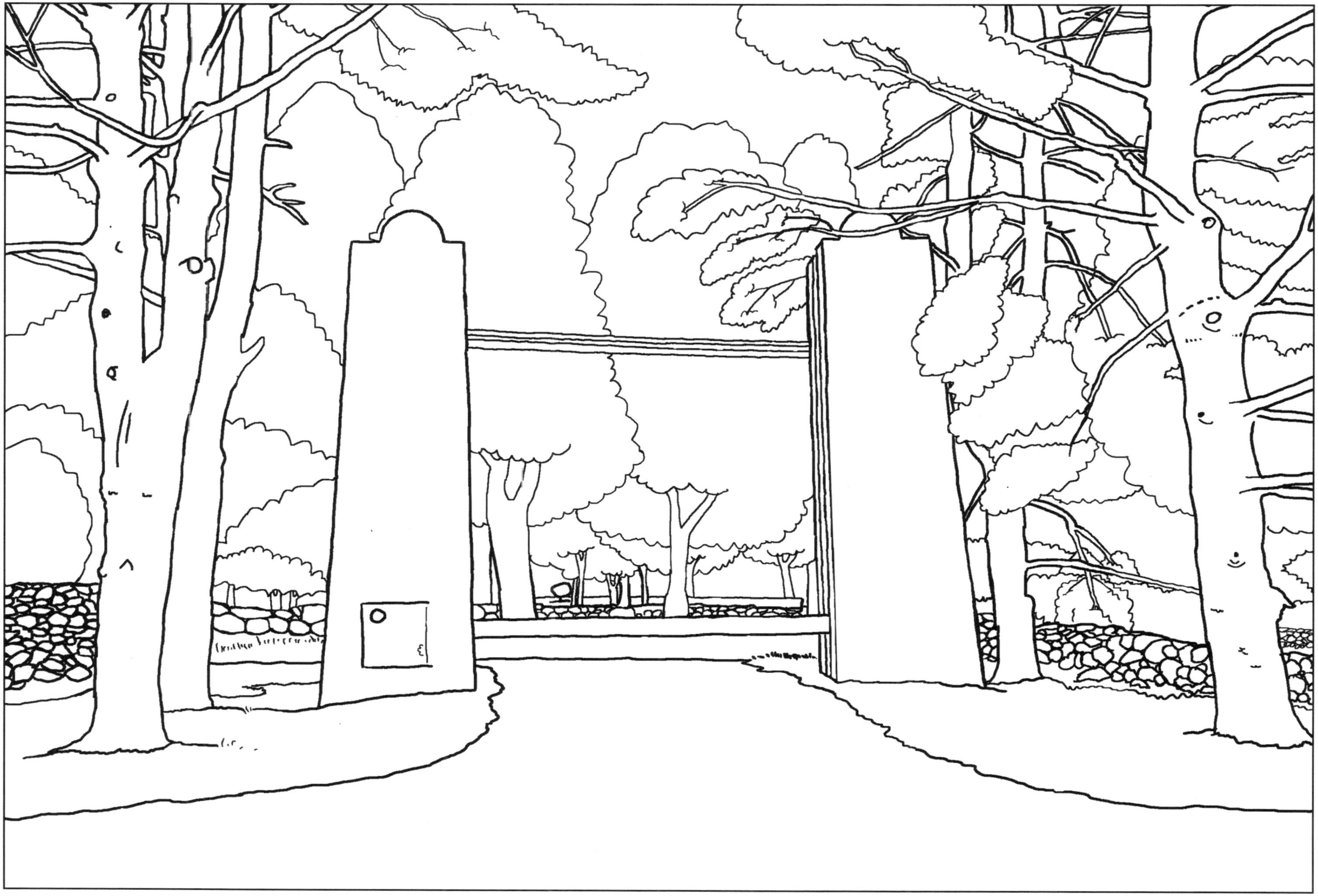

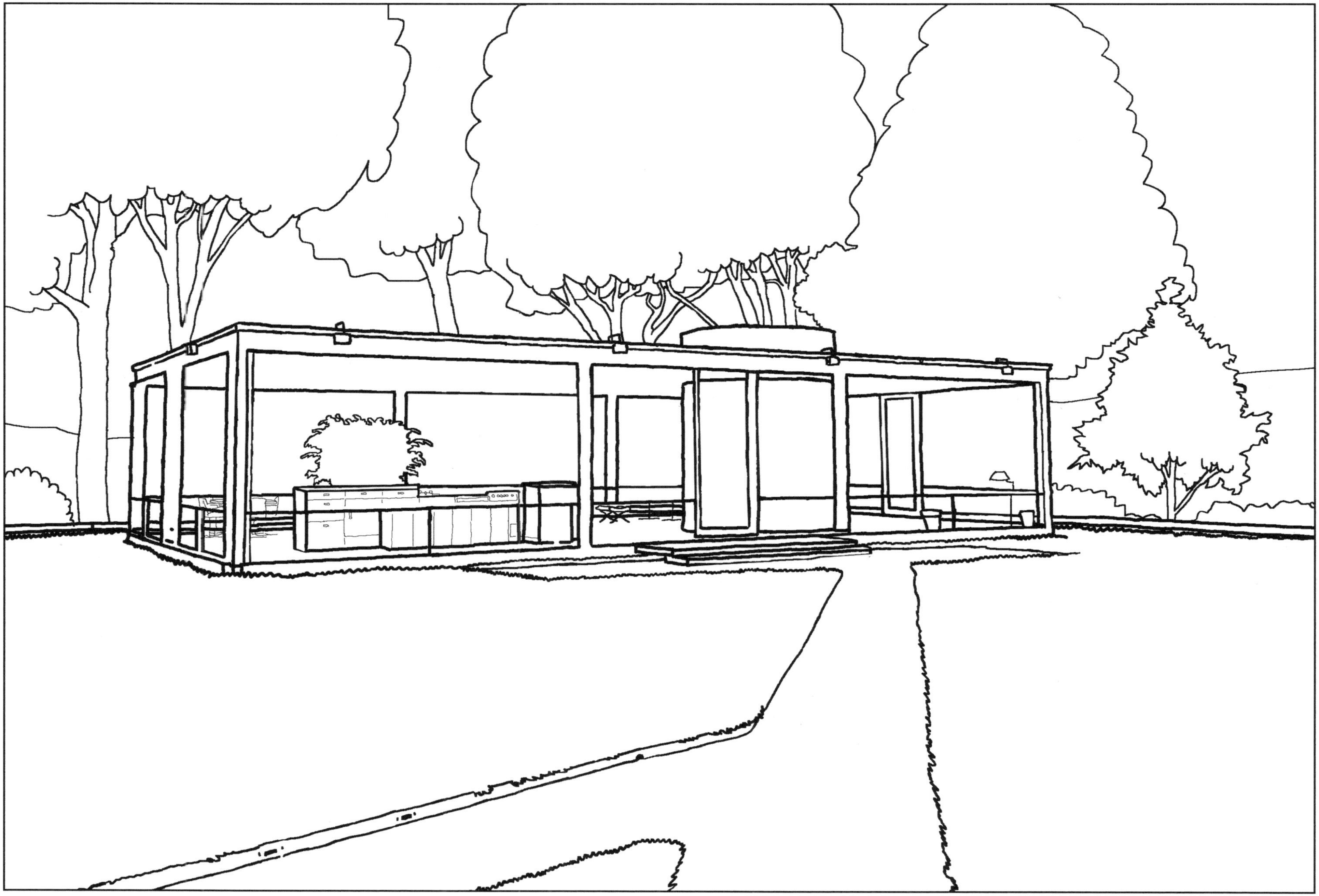

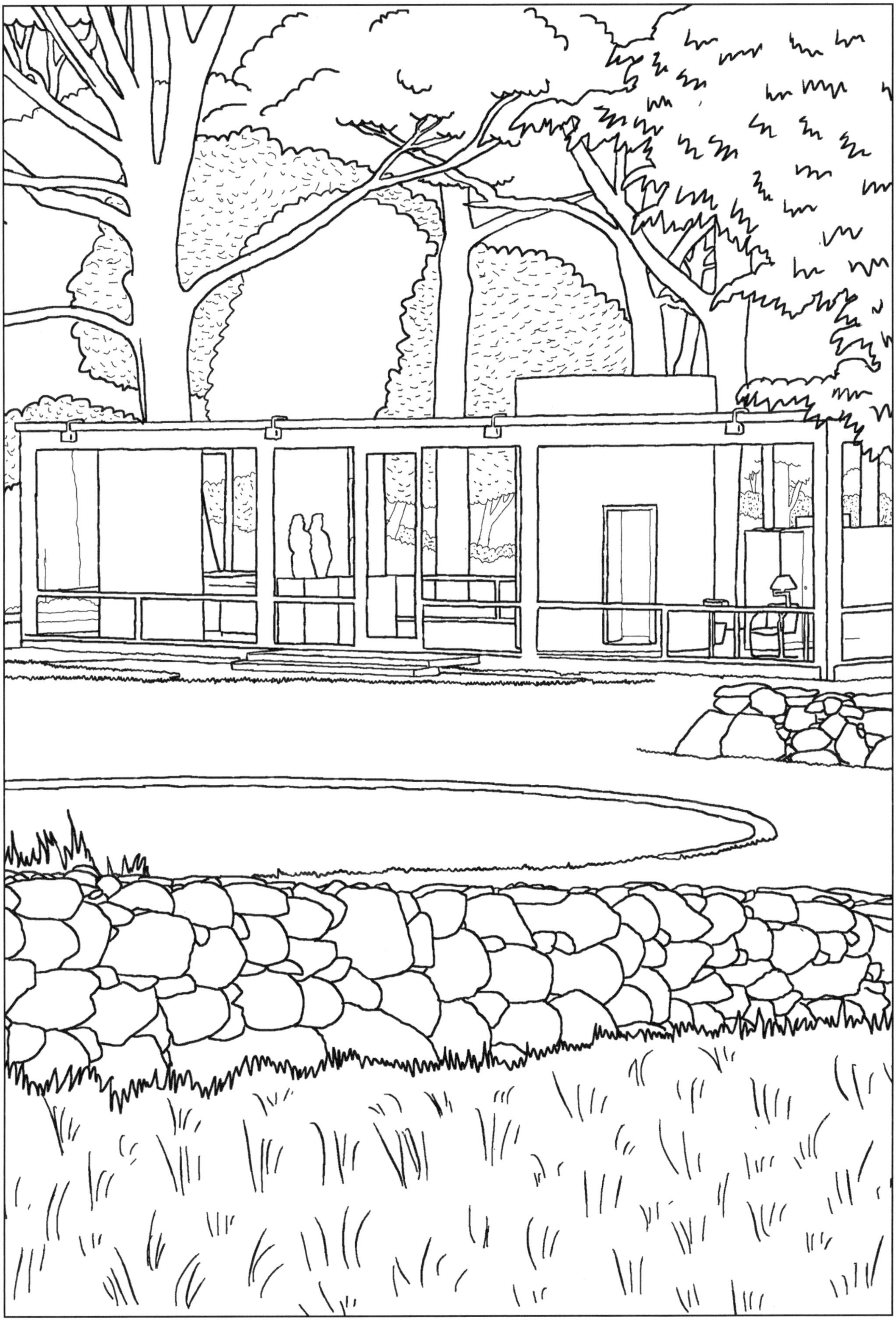

3. THE GLASS HOUSE AND POOL

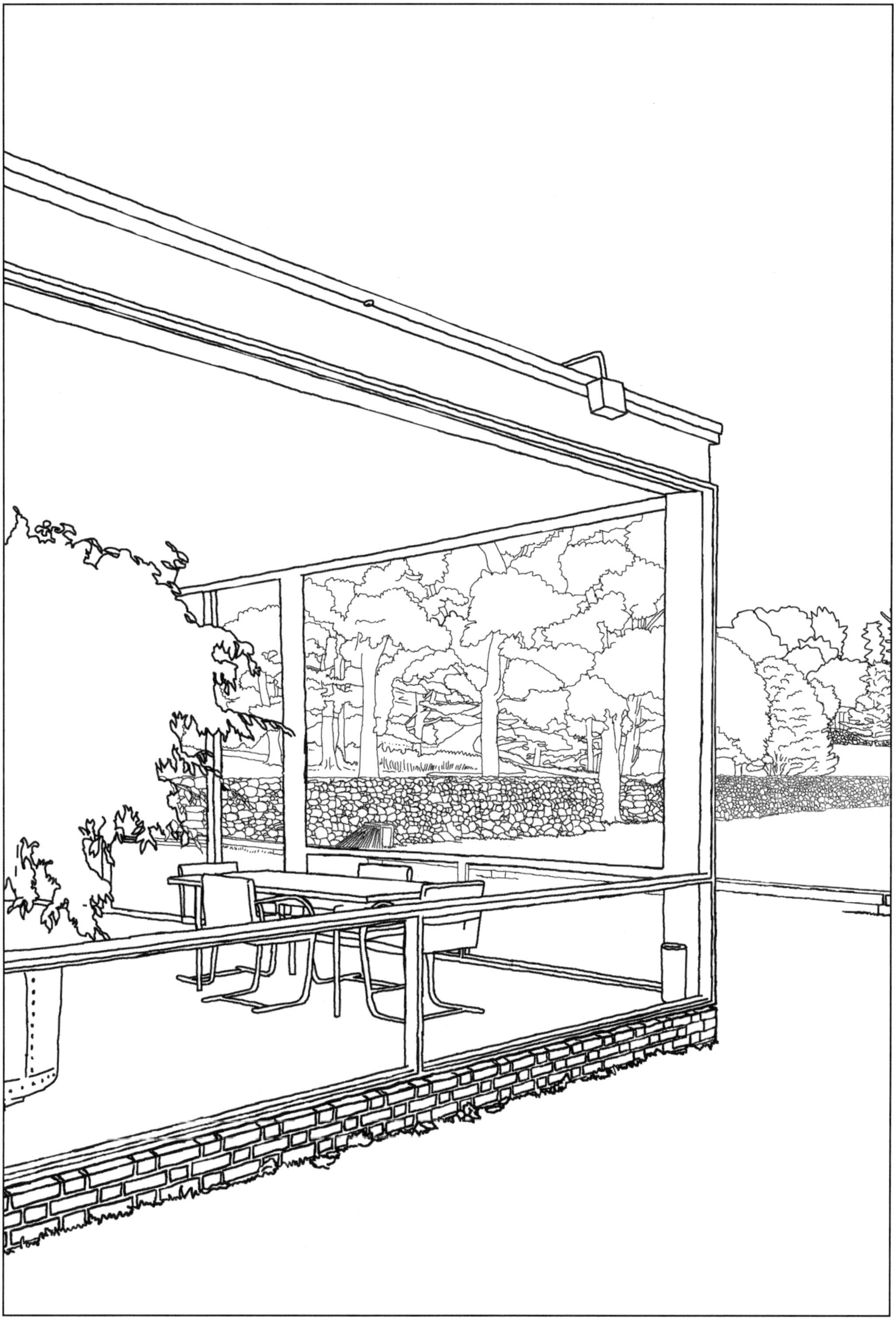

4. THE DINING AREA IN THE GLASS HOUSE

5. THE LIVING ROOM IN THE GLASS HOUSE

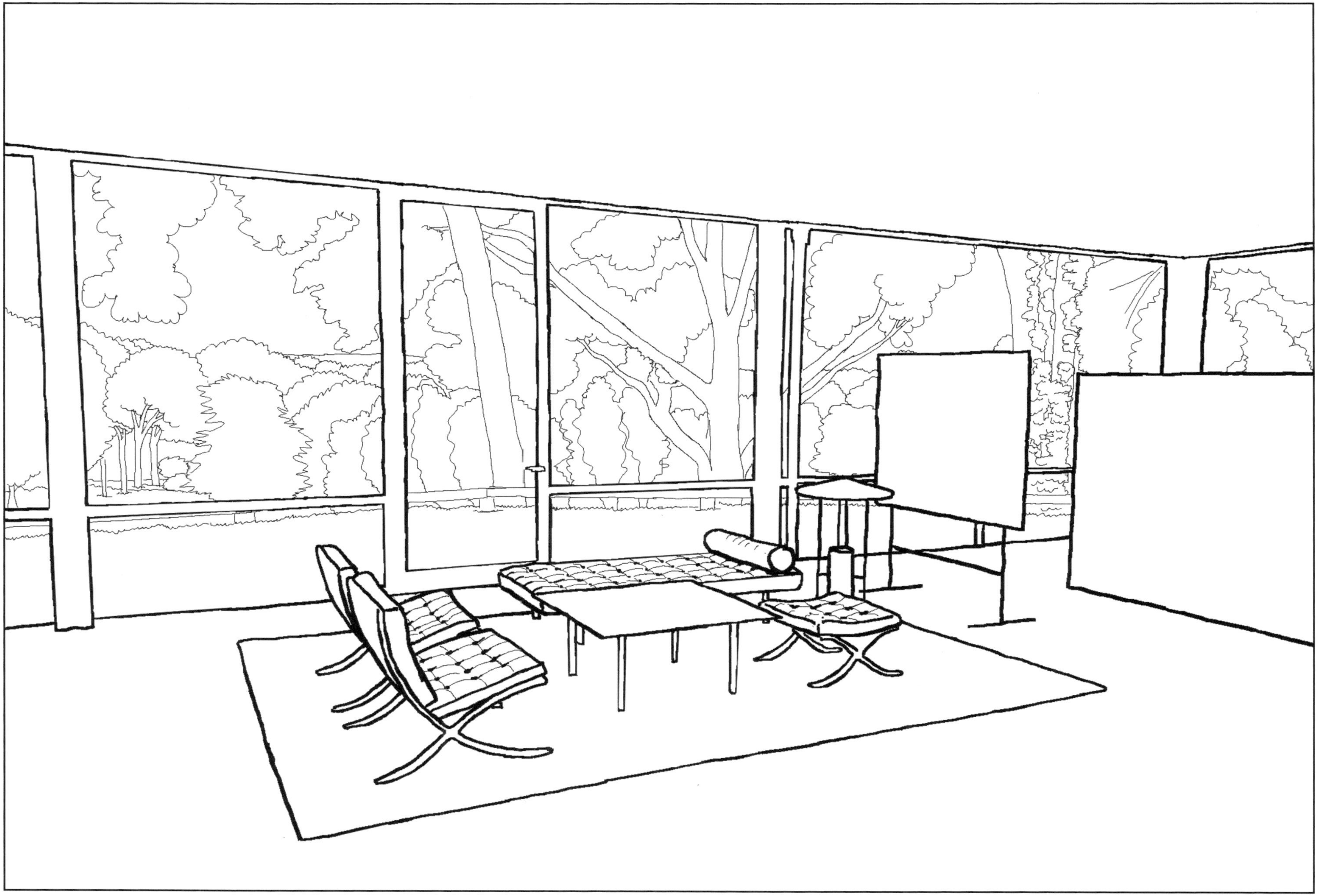

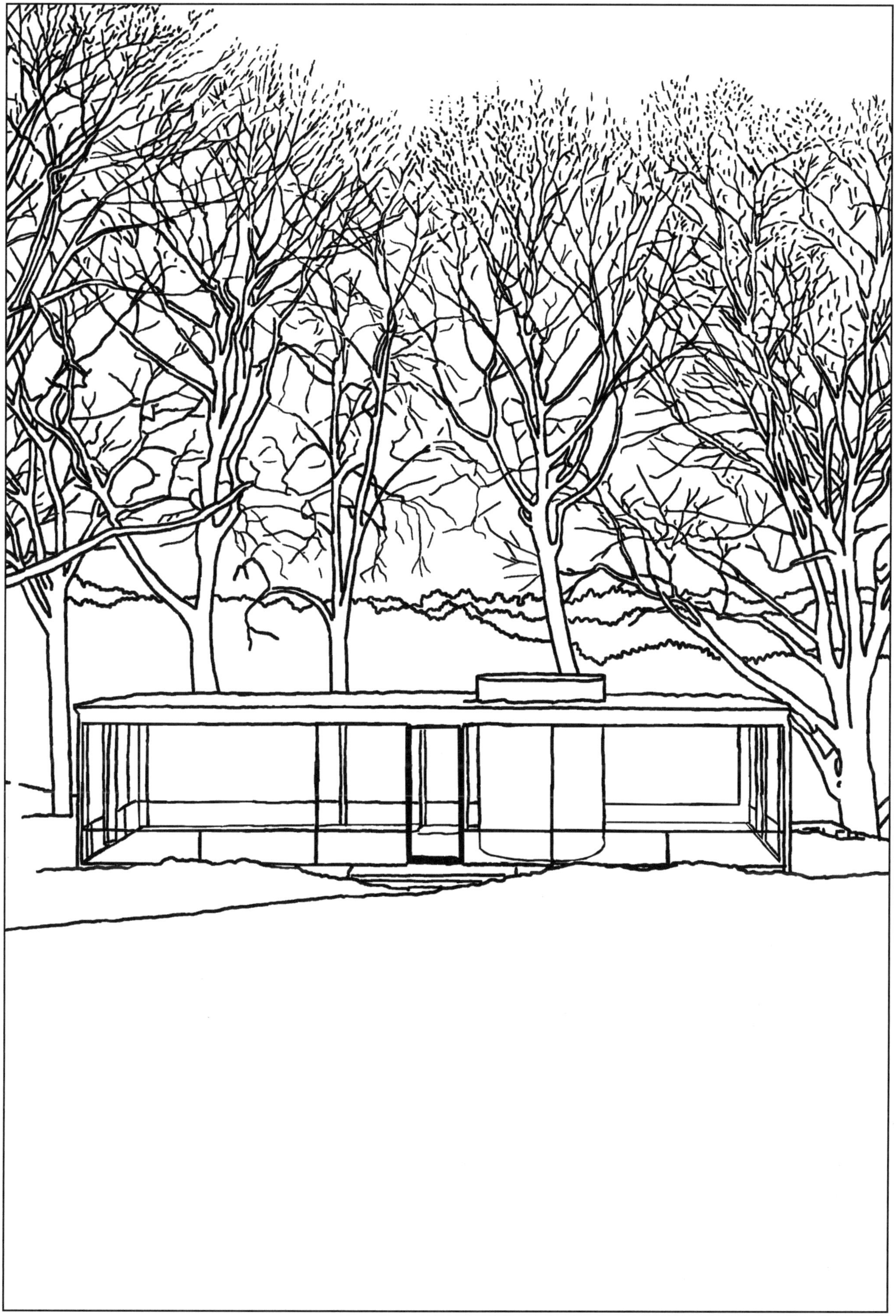

6. THE GLASS HOUSE IN WINTER

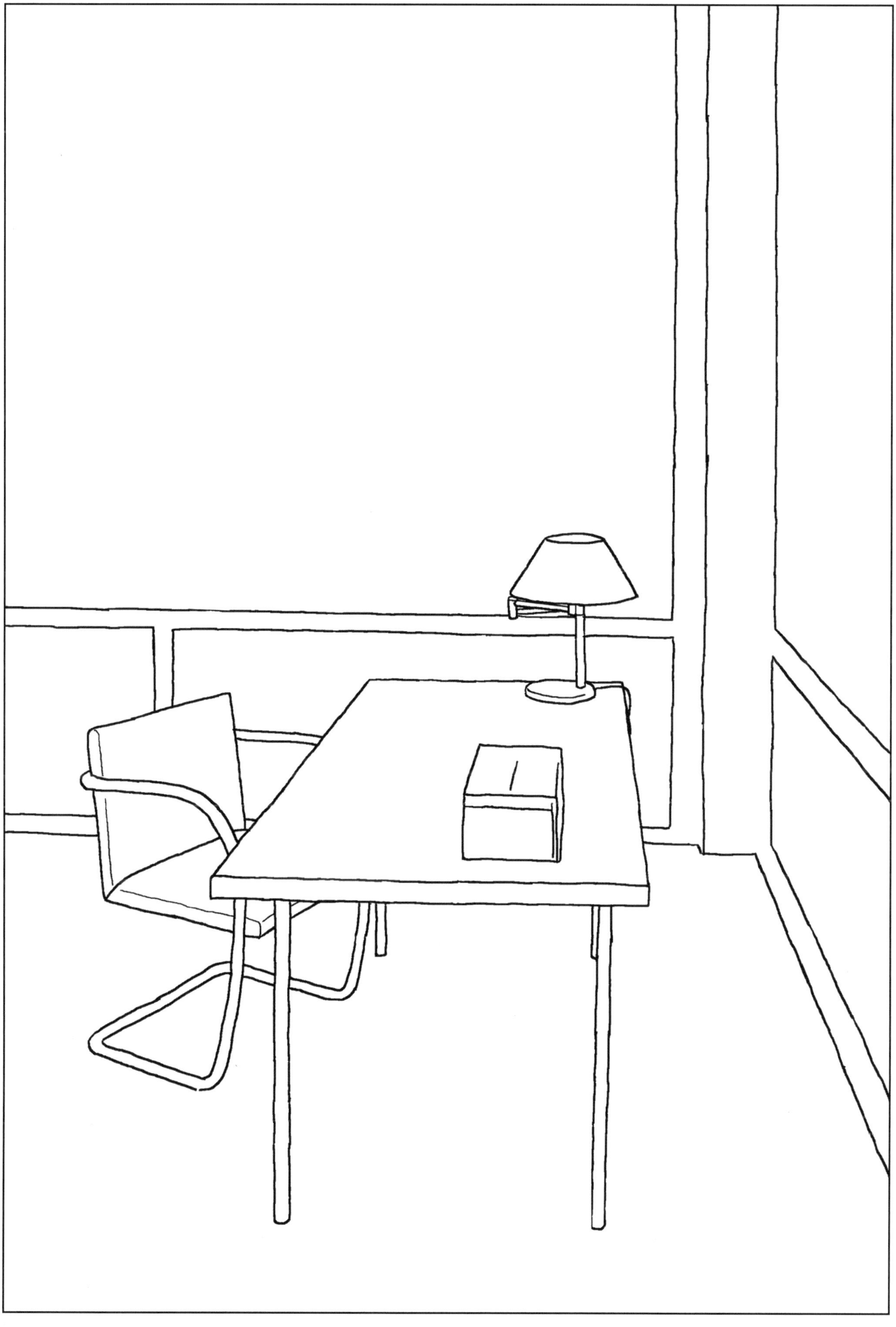

7. THE STUDY IN THE GLASS HOUSE

8. THE GLASS HOUSE AND ITS SURROUNDINGS

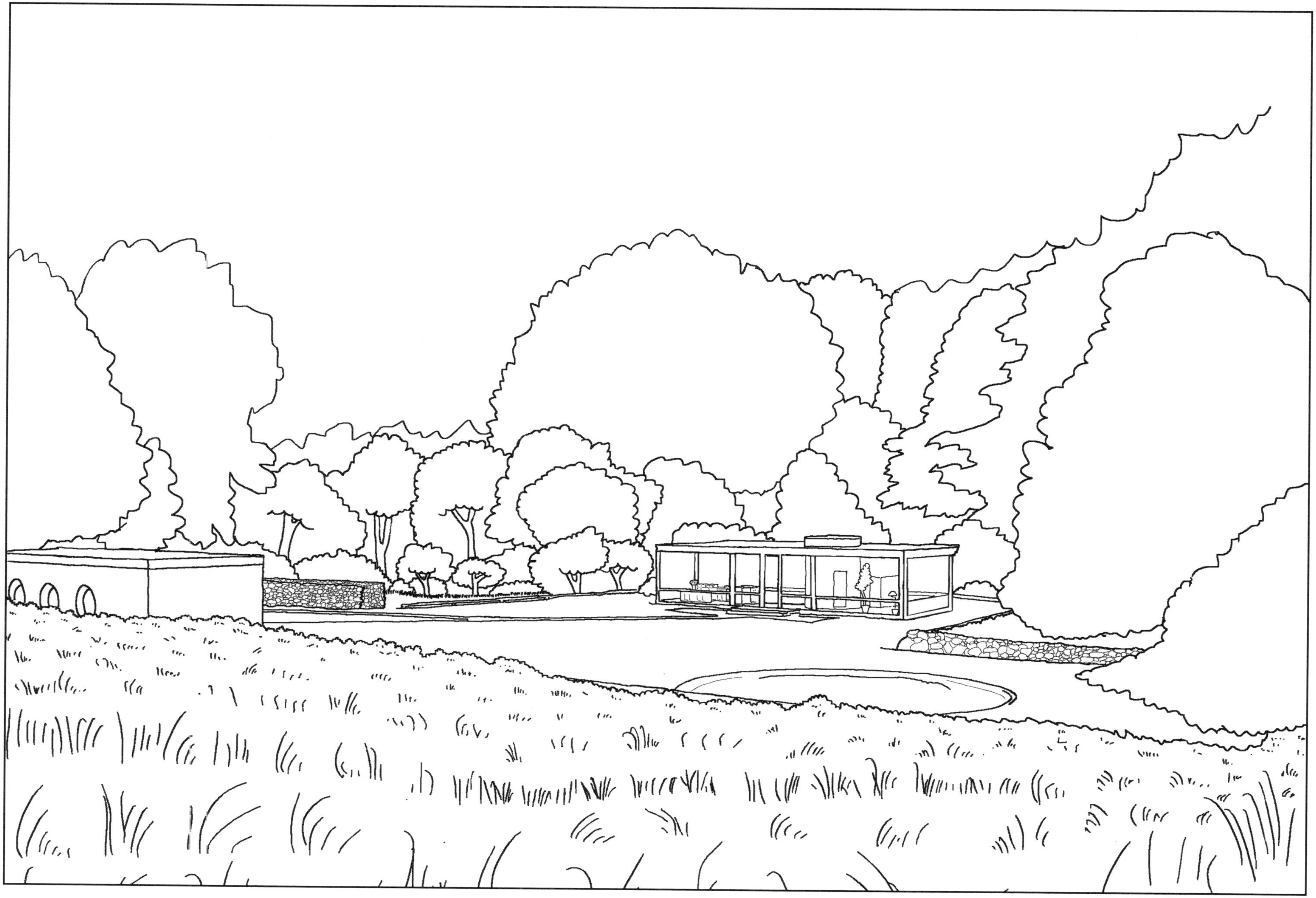

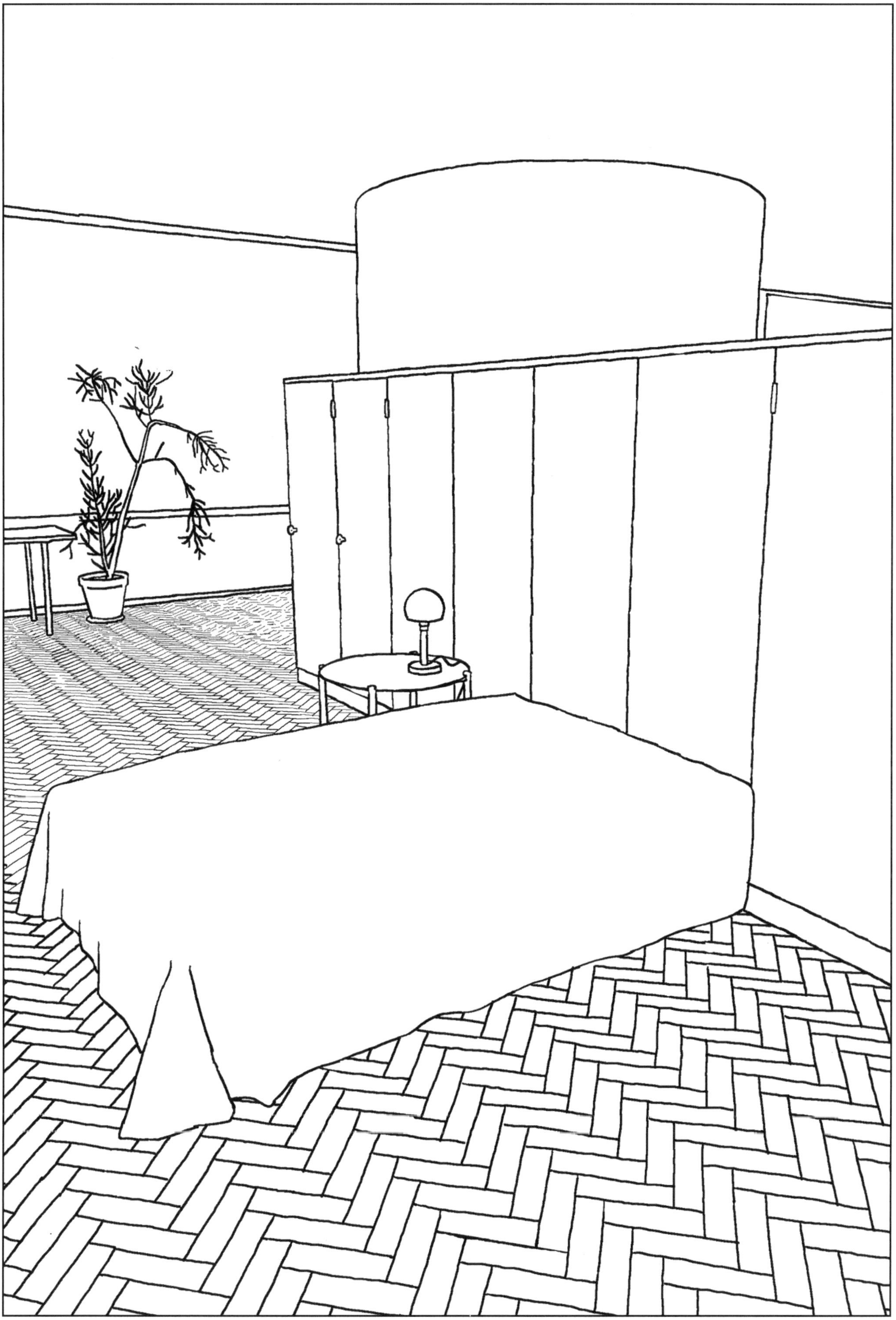

9. THE BEDROOM IN THE GLASS HOUSE

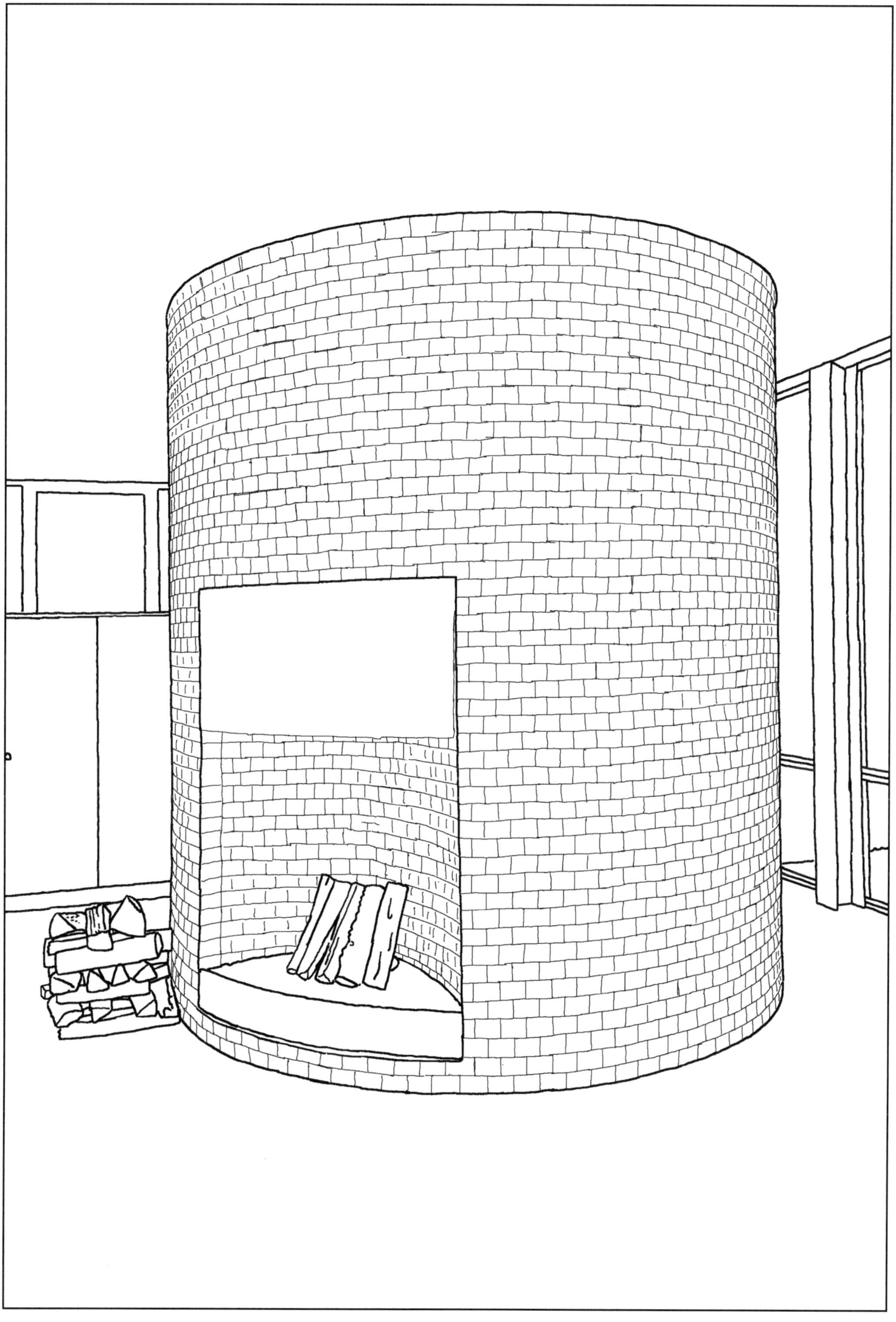

10. THE BRICK FIREPLACE IN THE GLASS HOUSE

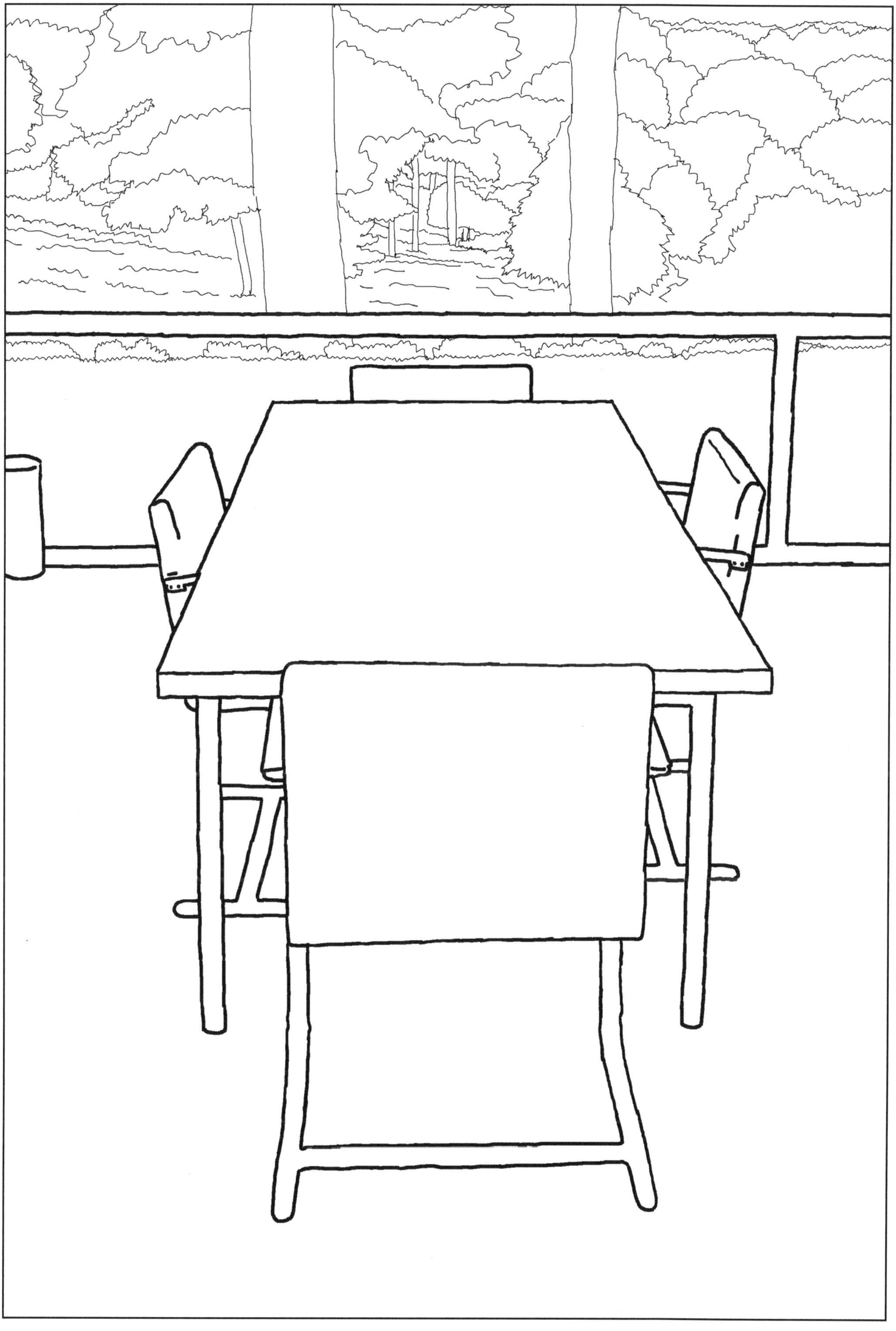

11. BRNO CHAIRS BY LUDWIG MIES VAN DER ROHE IN THE DINING AREA

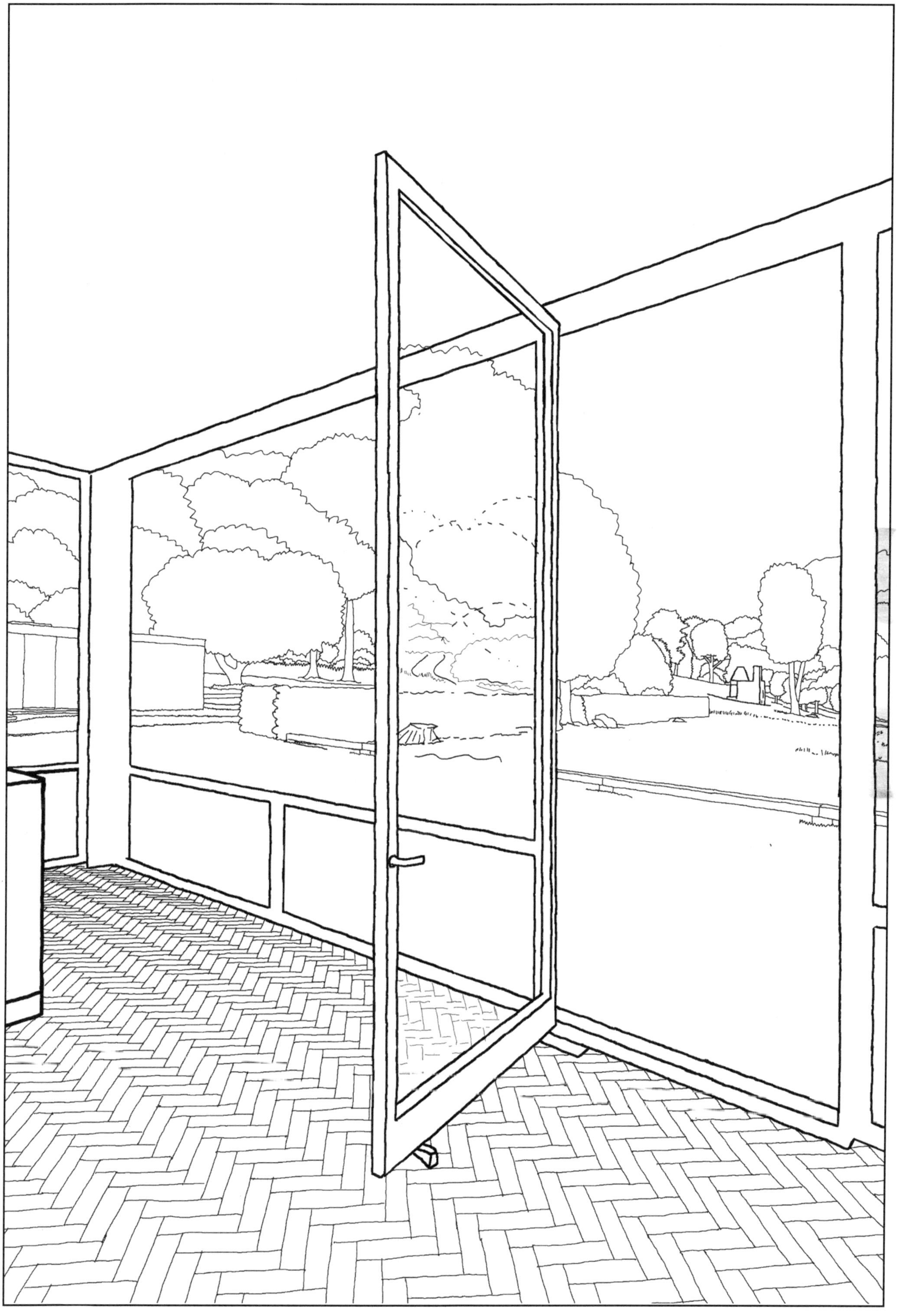

12. A GLASS DOOR IN A GLASS WALL

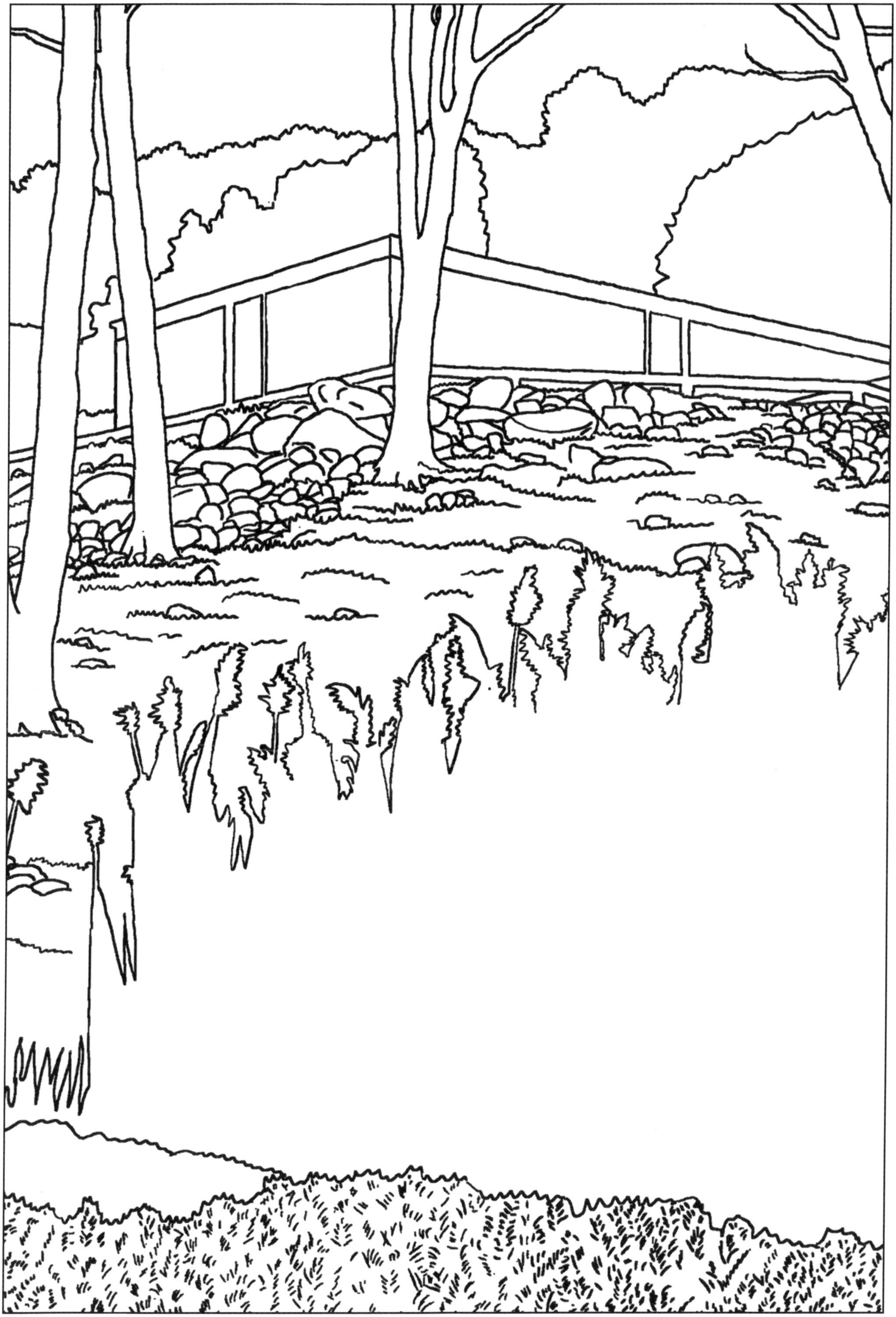

13. THE GLASS HOUSE AS SEEN FROM THE POND

14. THE BRICK HOUSE

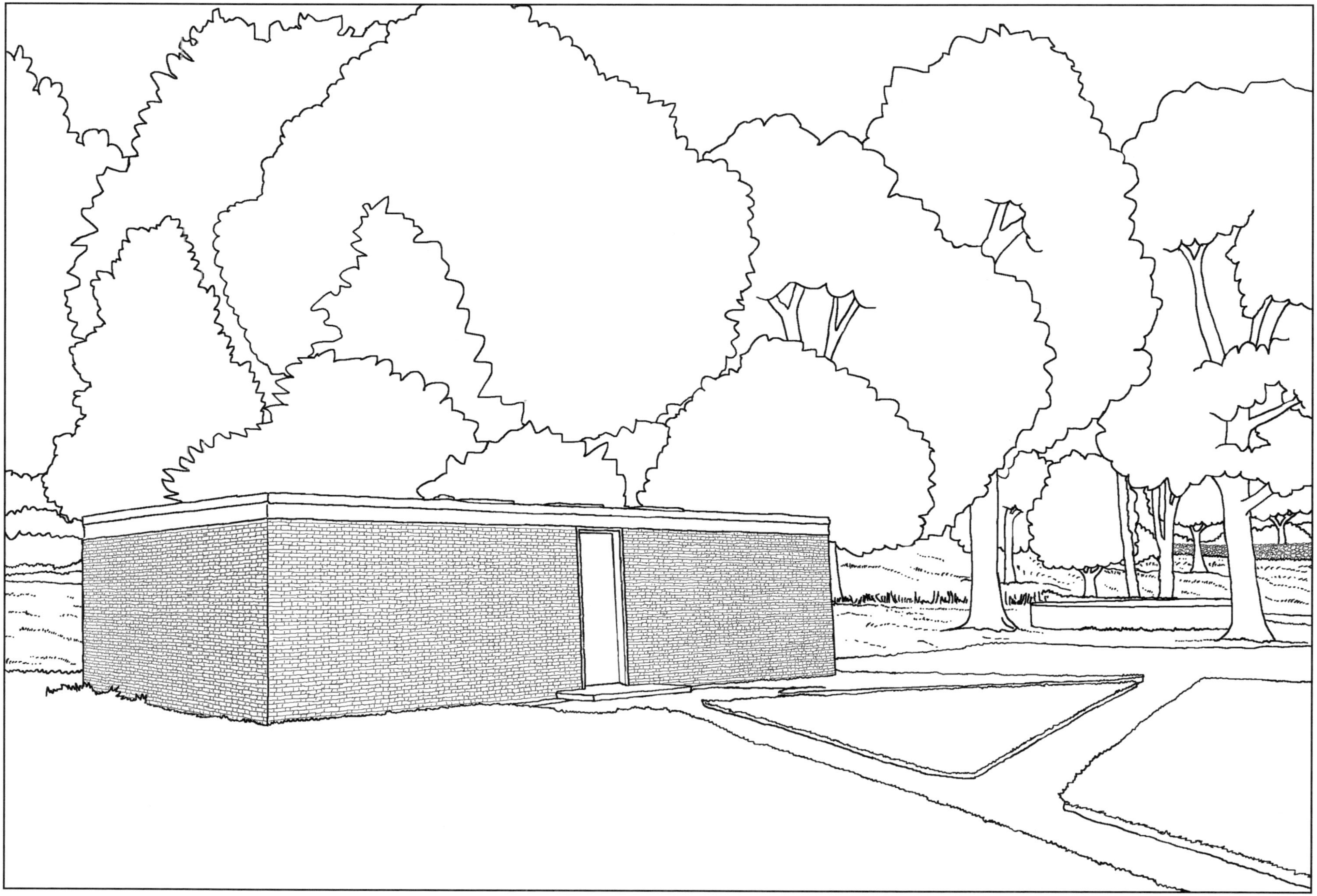

15. THE PAVILION IN THE POND

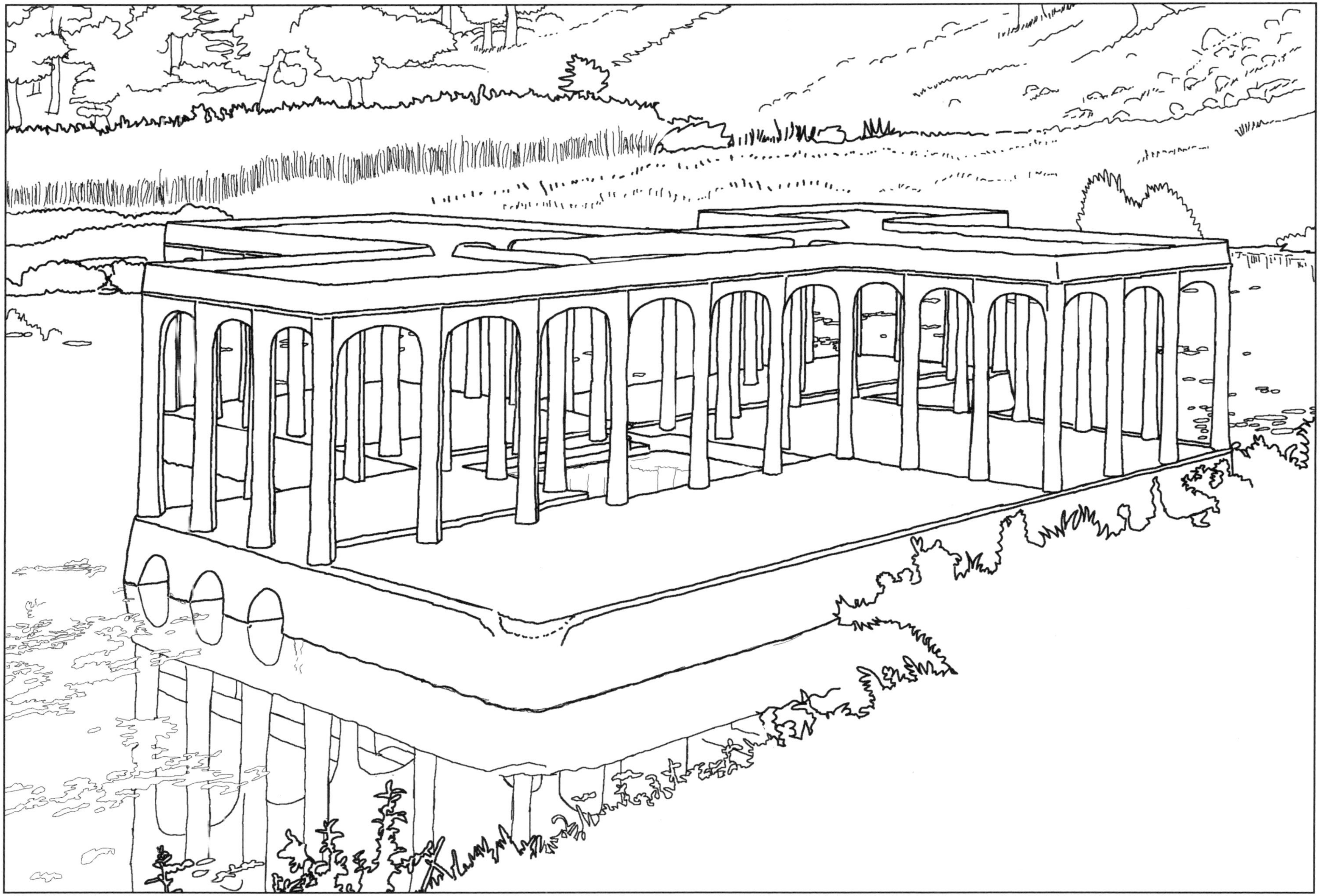

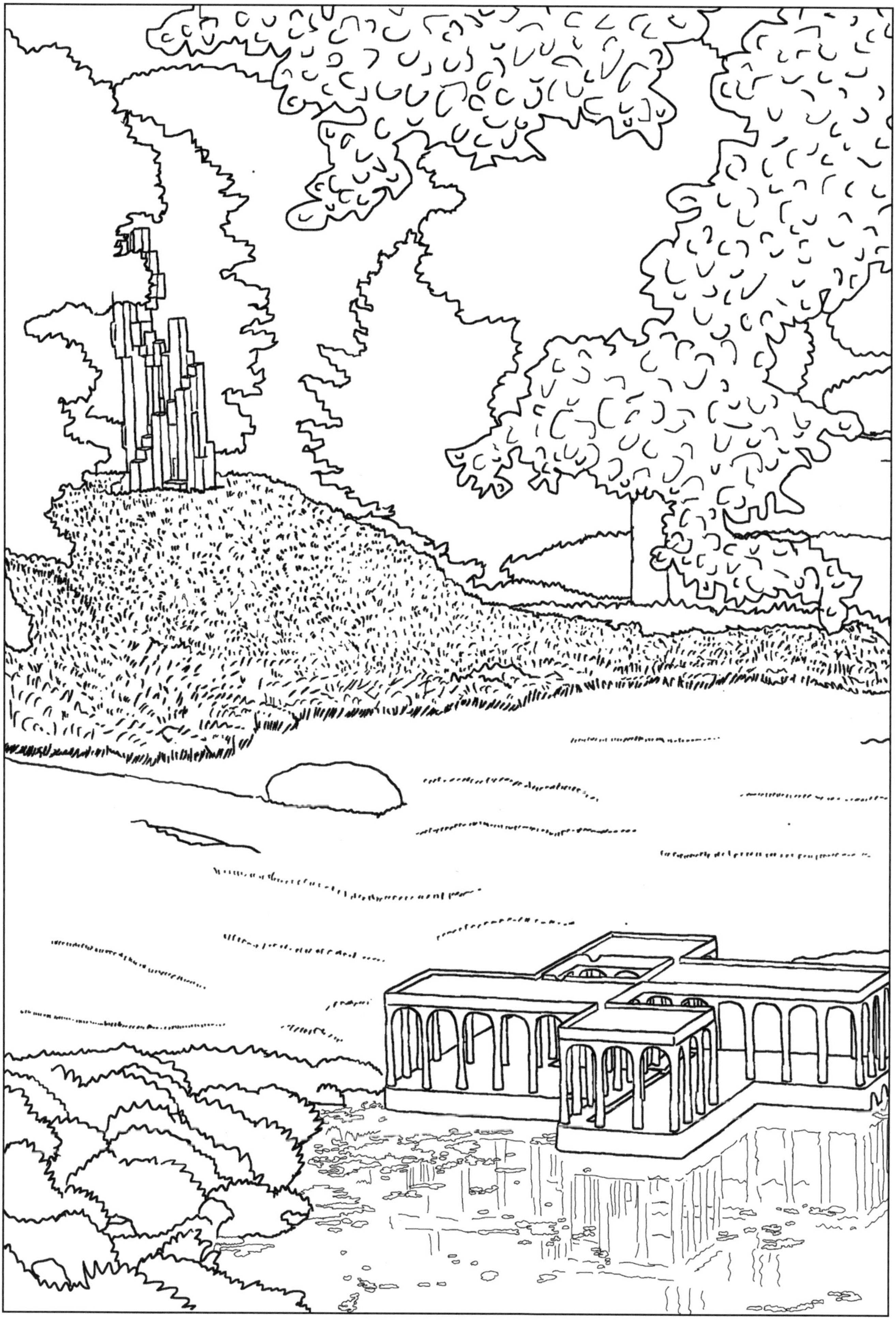

16. THE PAVILION IN THE POND AND THE MONUMENT TO LINCOLN KIRSTEIN IN THE BACKGROUND

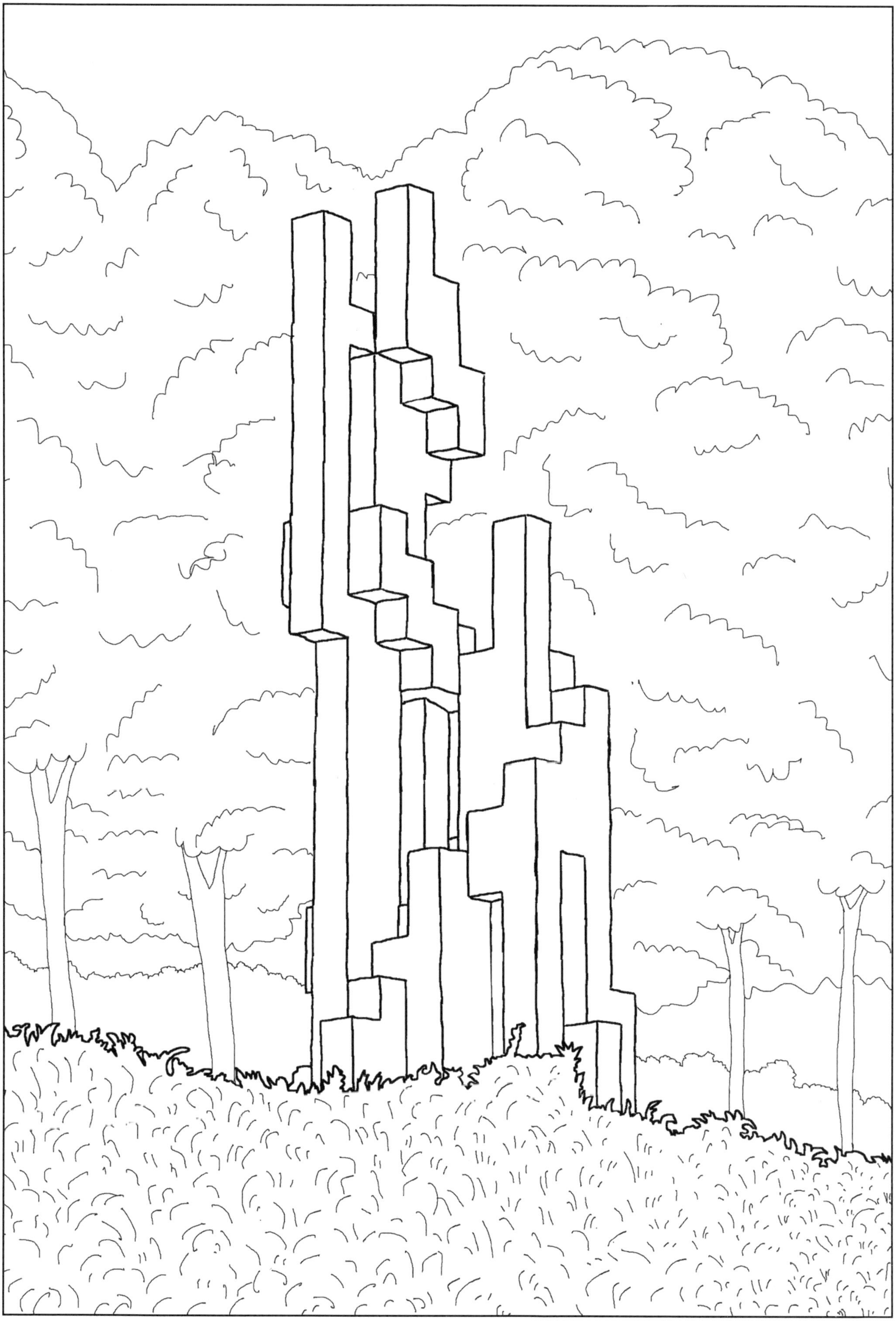

17. THE MONUMENT TO LINCOLN KIRSTEIN

18. THE SCULPTURE GALLERY EXTERIOR

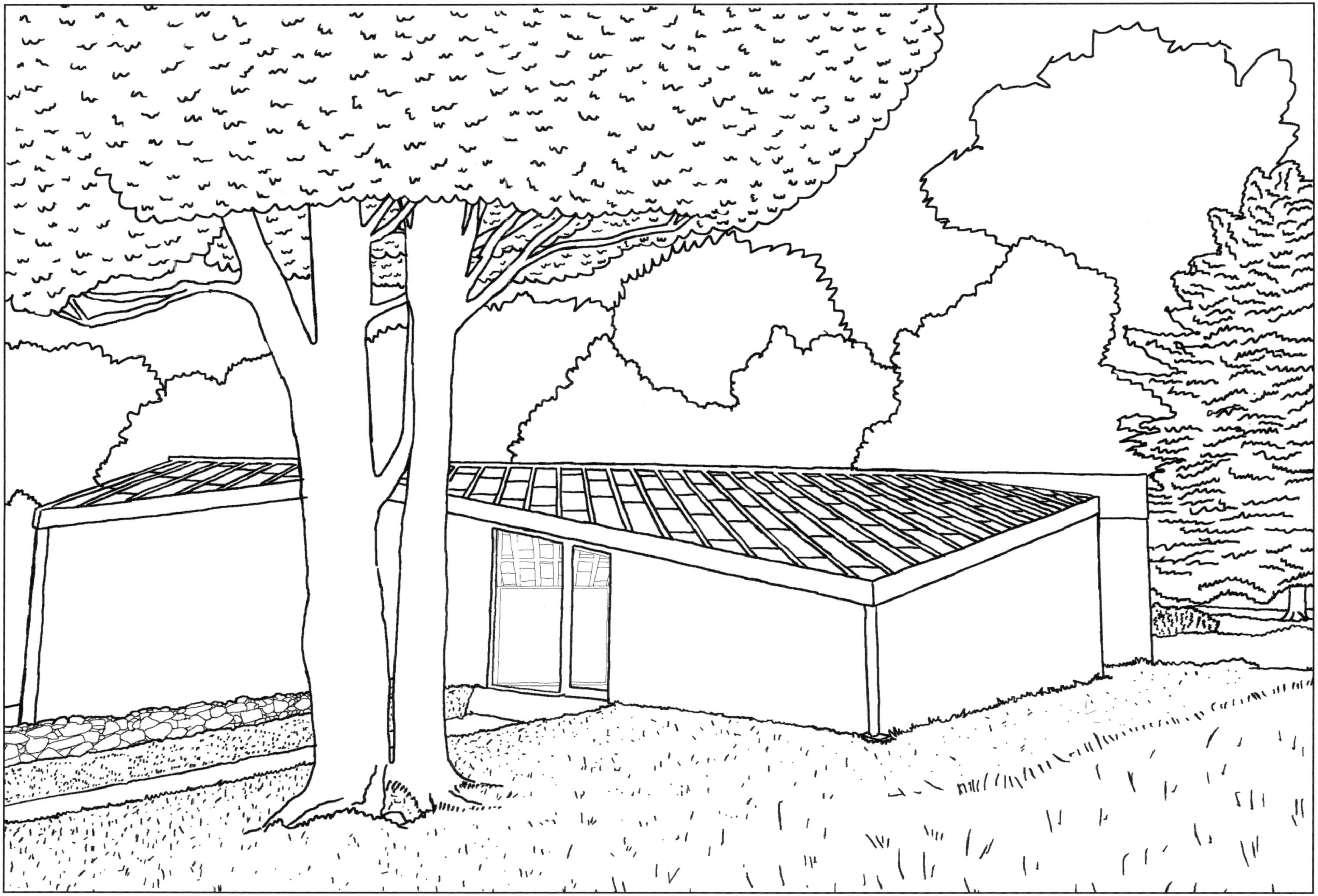

19. ROBERT MORRIS SCULPTURE AND PIECES BY ANDREW LORD IN THE SCULPTURE GALLERY

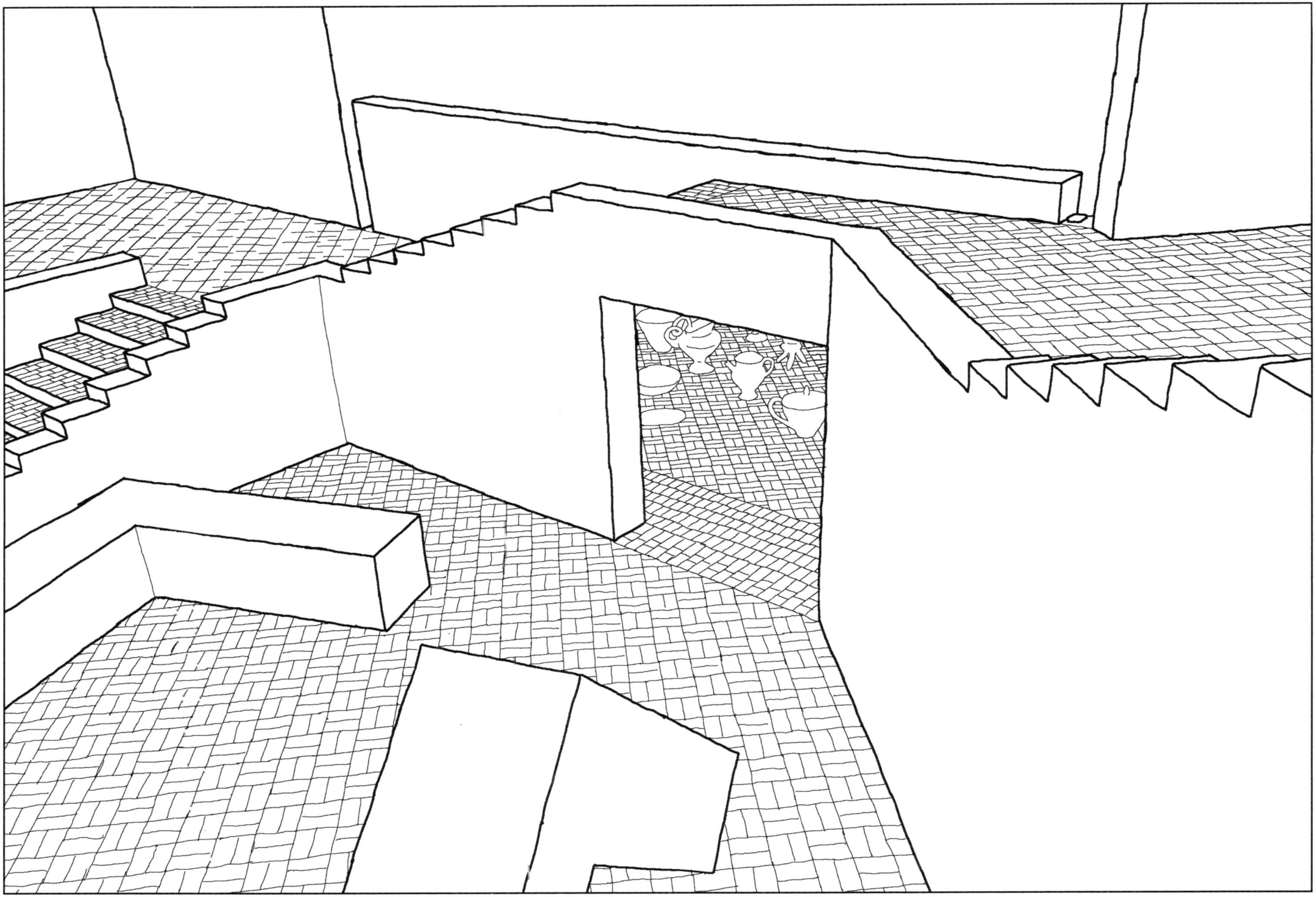

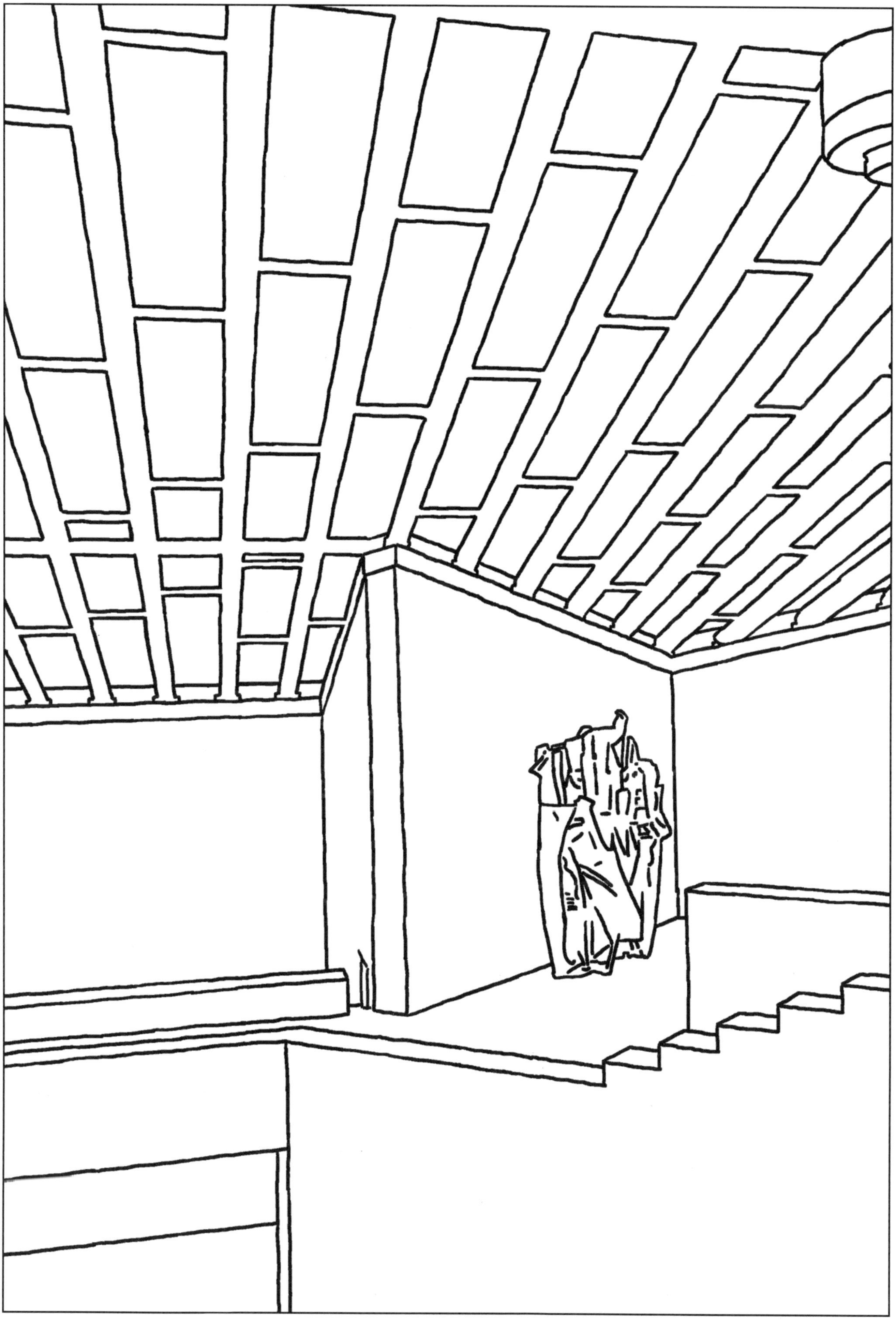

20. A JOHN CHAMBERLAIN SCULPTURE IN THE SCULPTURE GALLERY

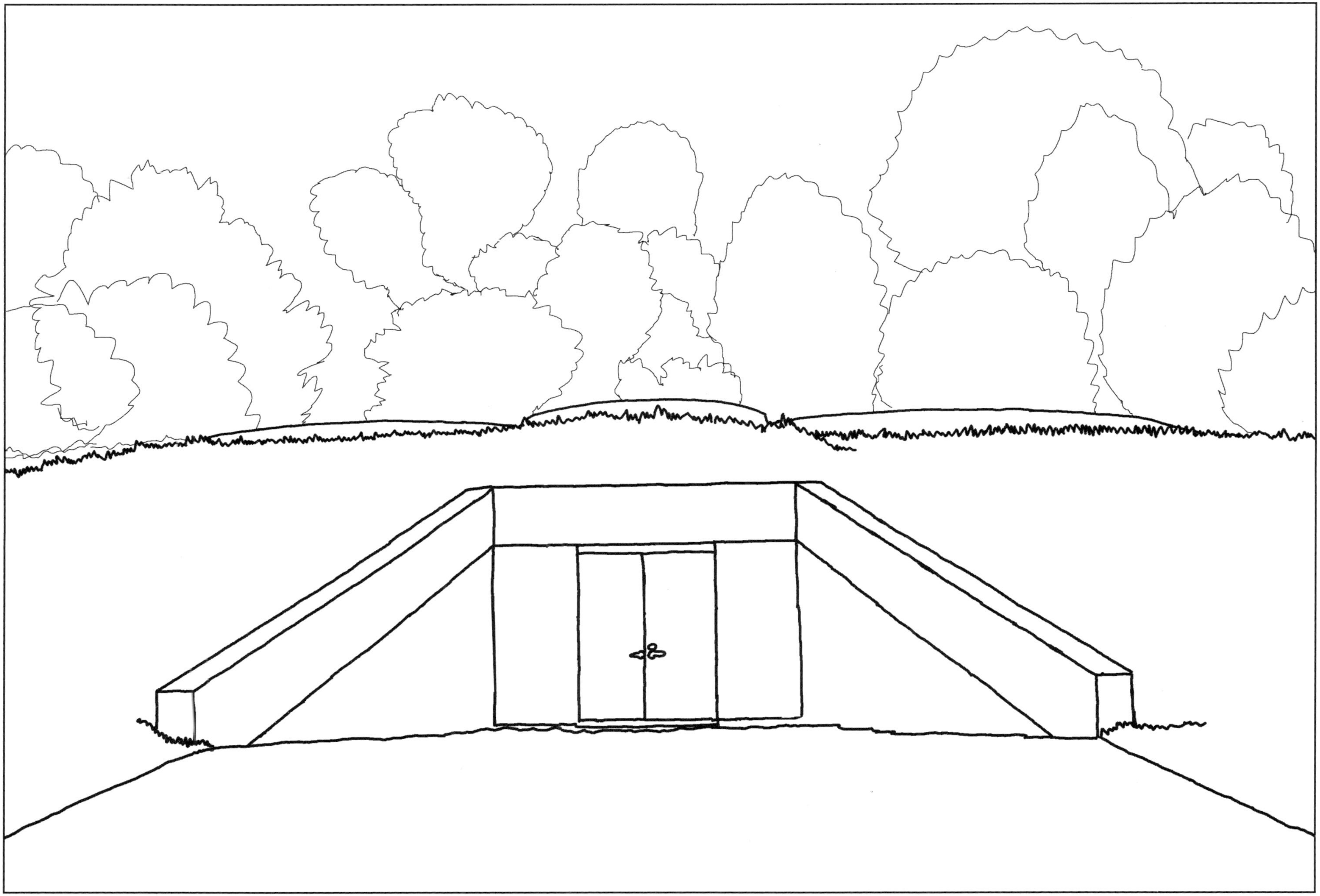

22. AN ANDY WARHOL WORK IN THE PAINTING GALLERY

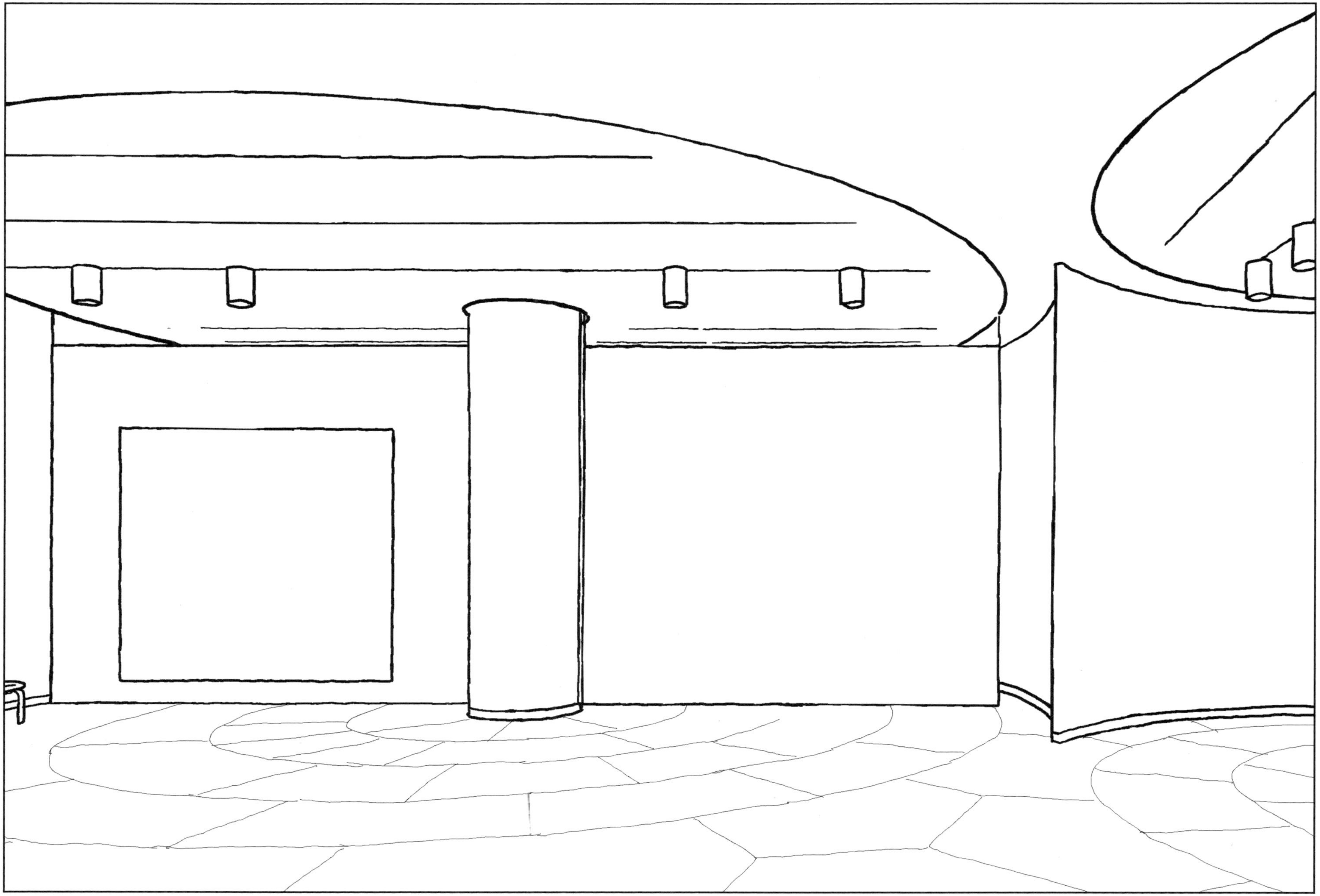

23. LYNN DAVIS PHOTOGRAFHS IN THE PAINTING GALLERY

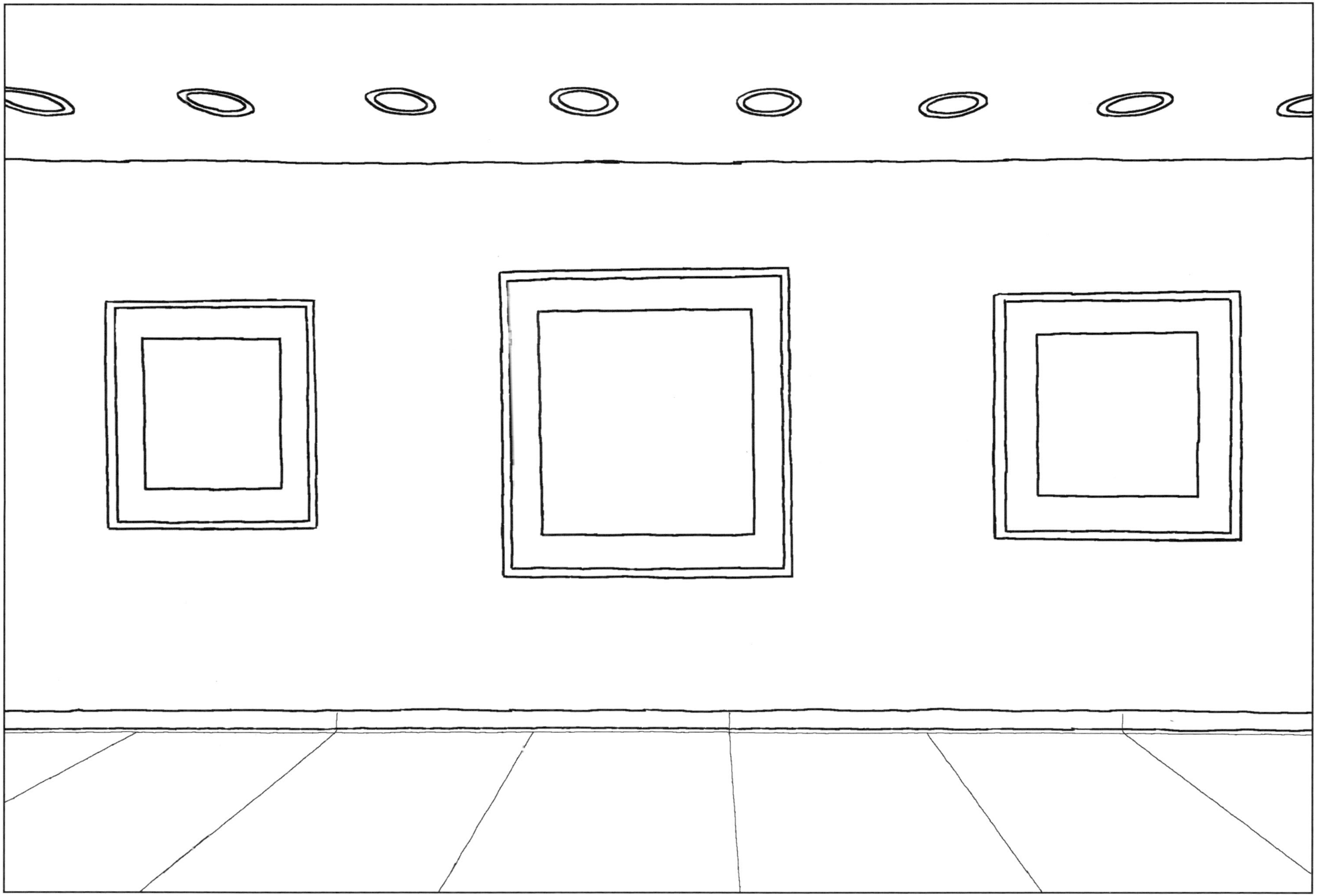

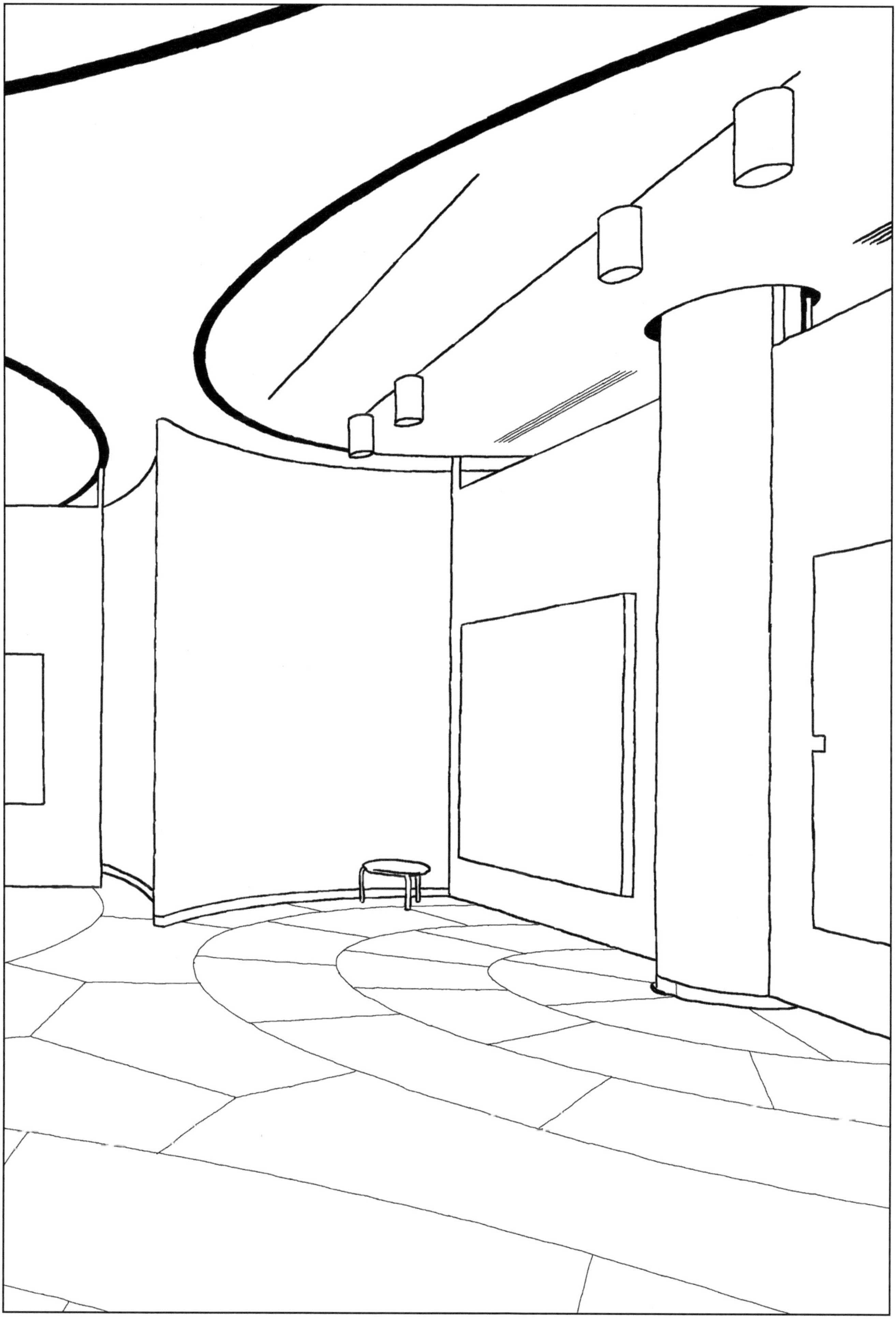

24. TWO FRANK STELLA PAINTINGS IN THE PAINTING GALLERY

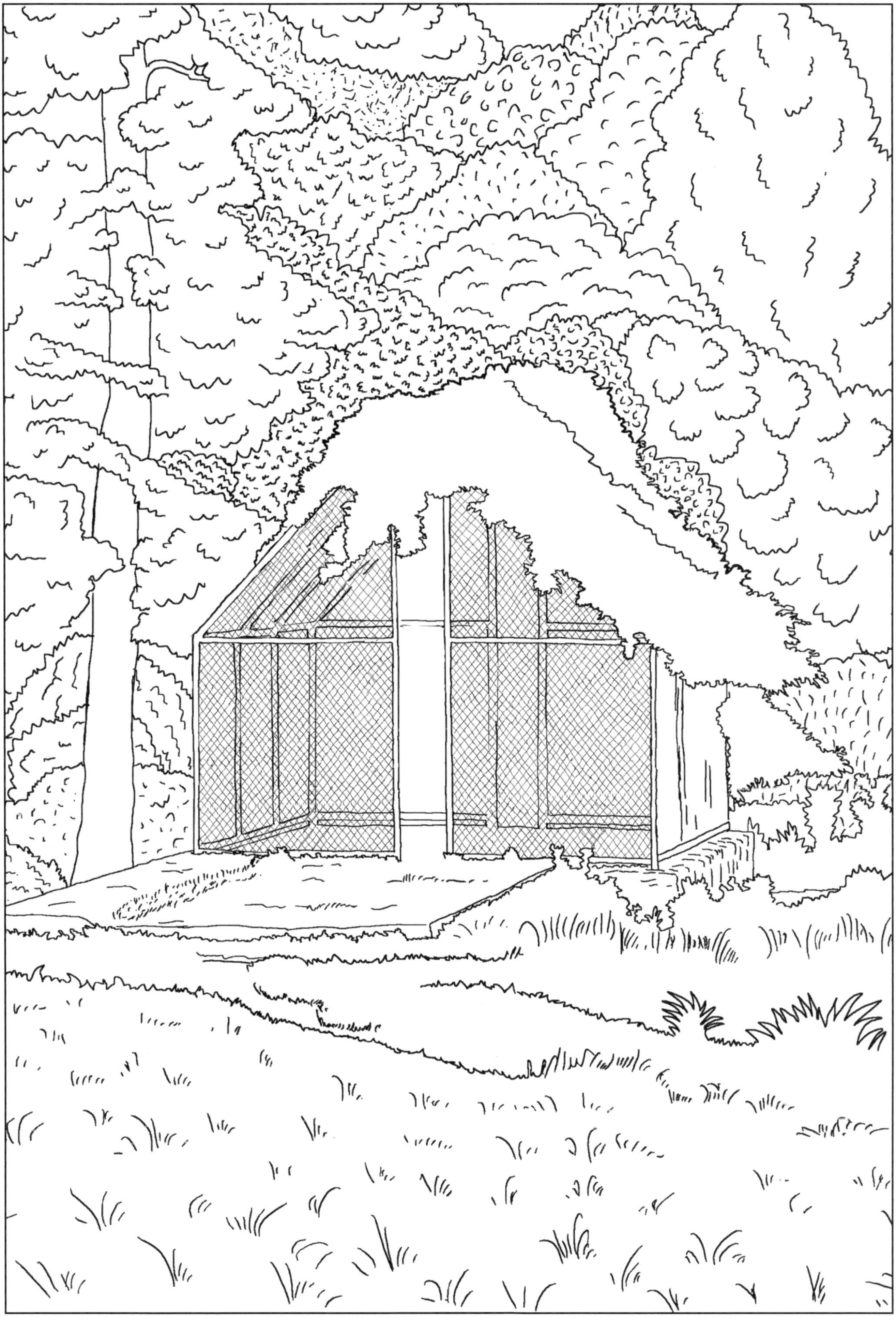

25. THE GHOST HOUSE

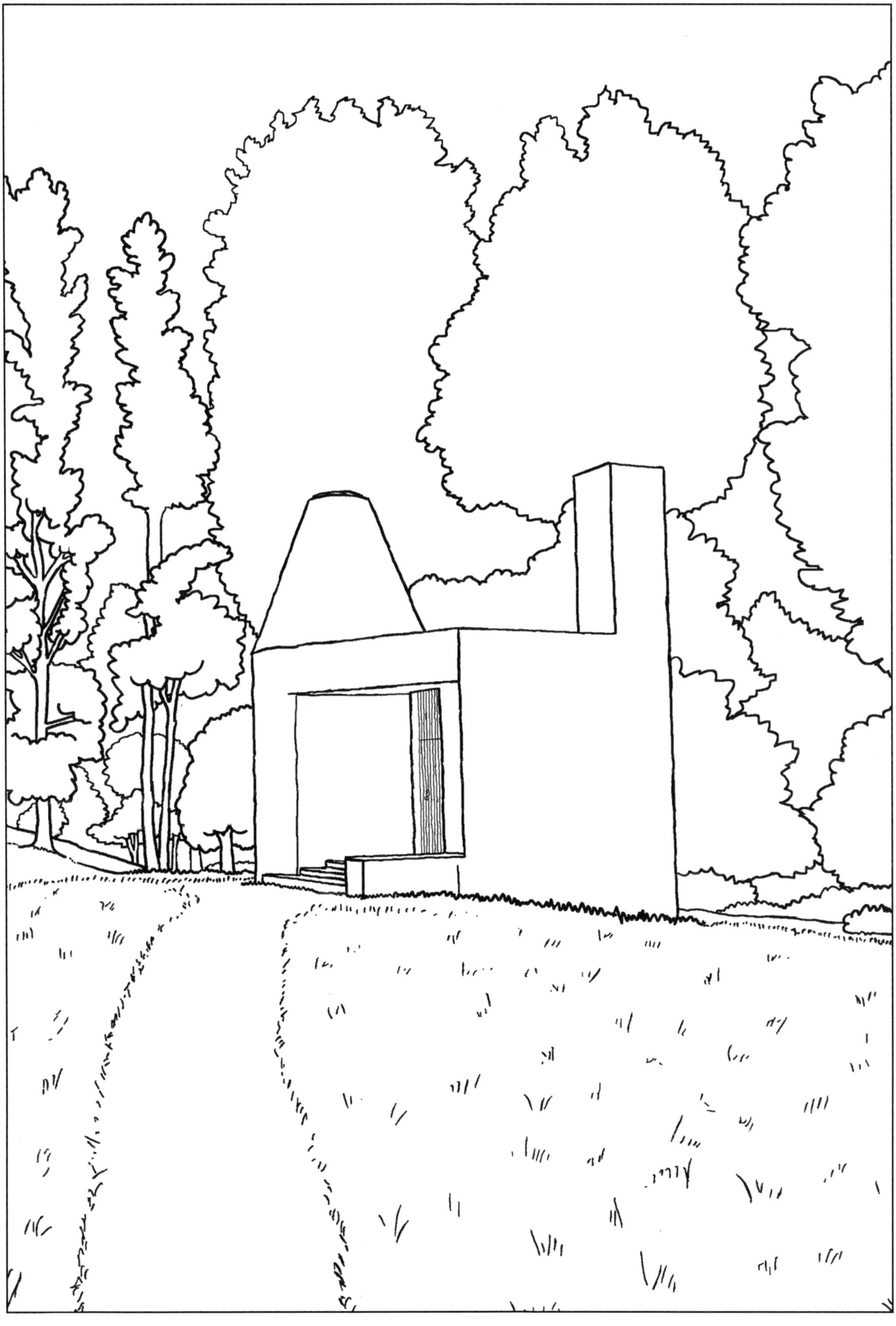

26. THE STUDIO EXTERICR

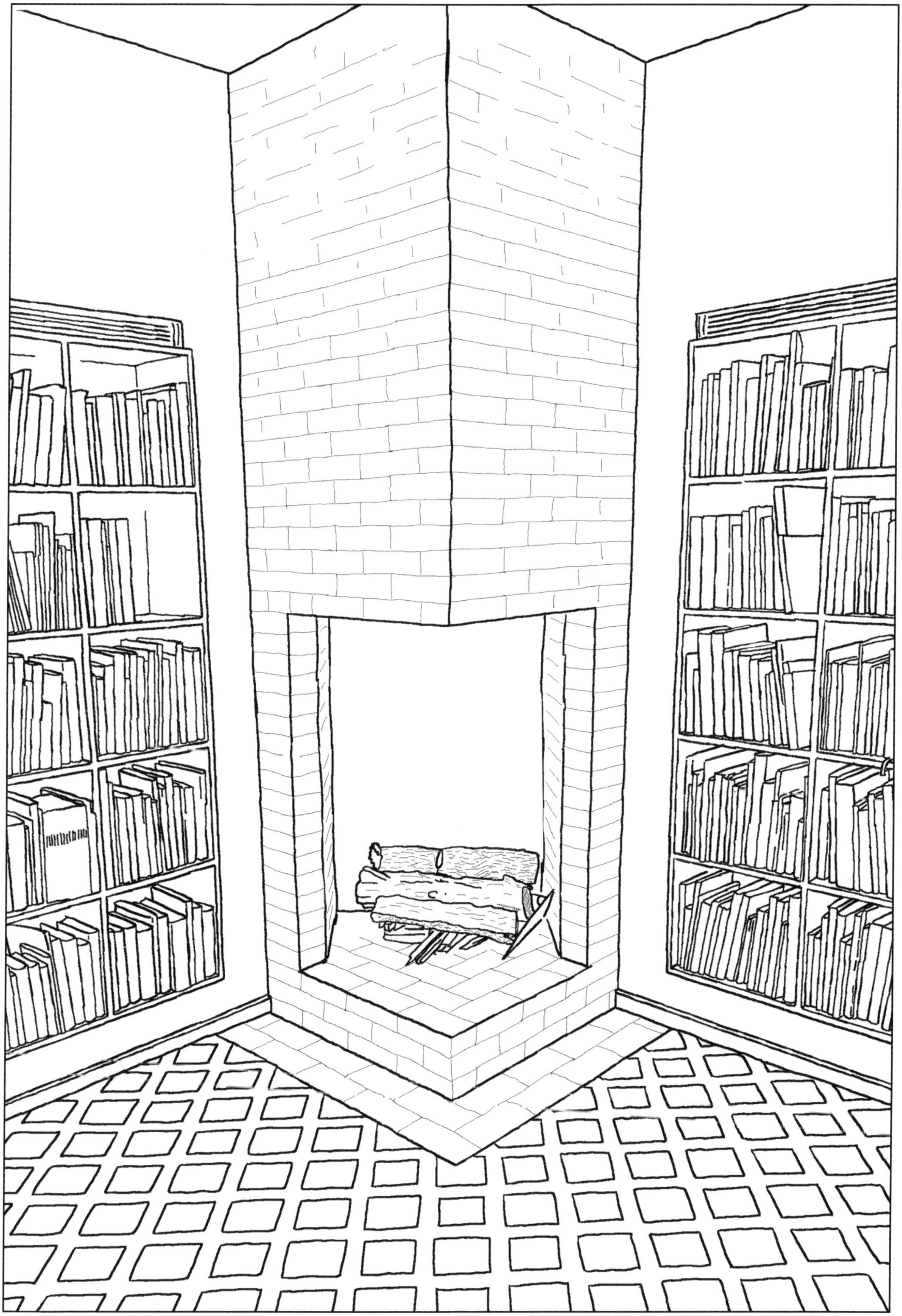

27. THE LIBRARY IN THE STUDIO

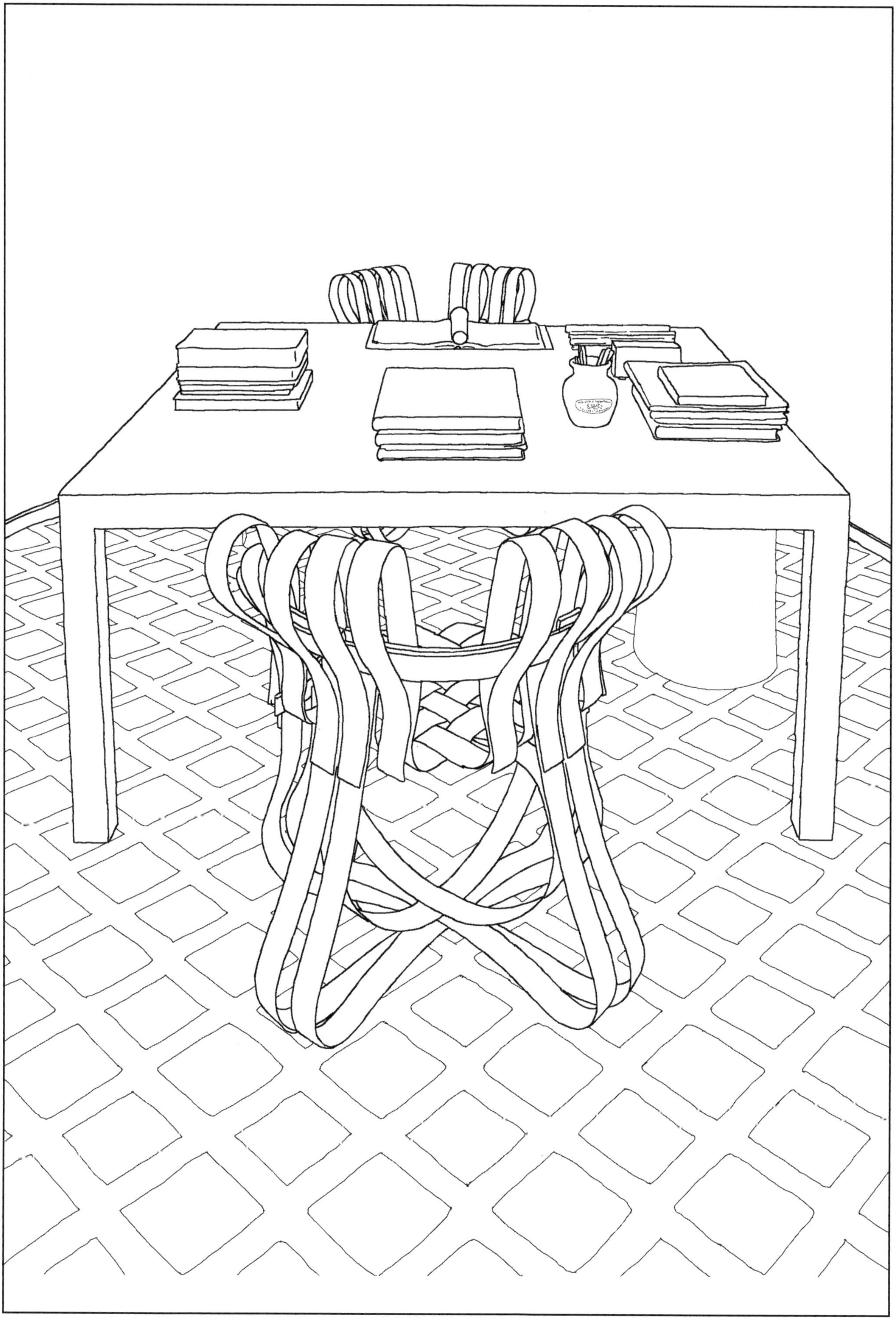

28. CHAIRS BY FRANK GEHRY FOR KNOLL IN THE STUDIO

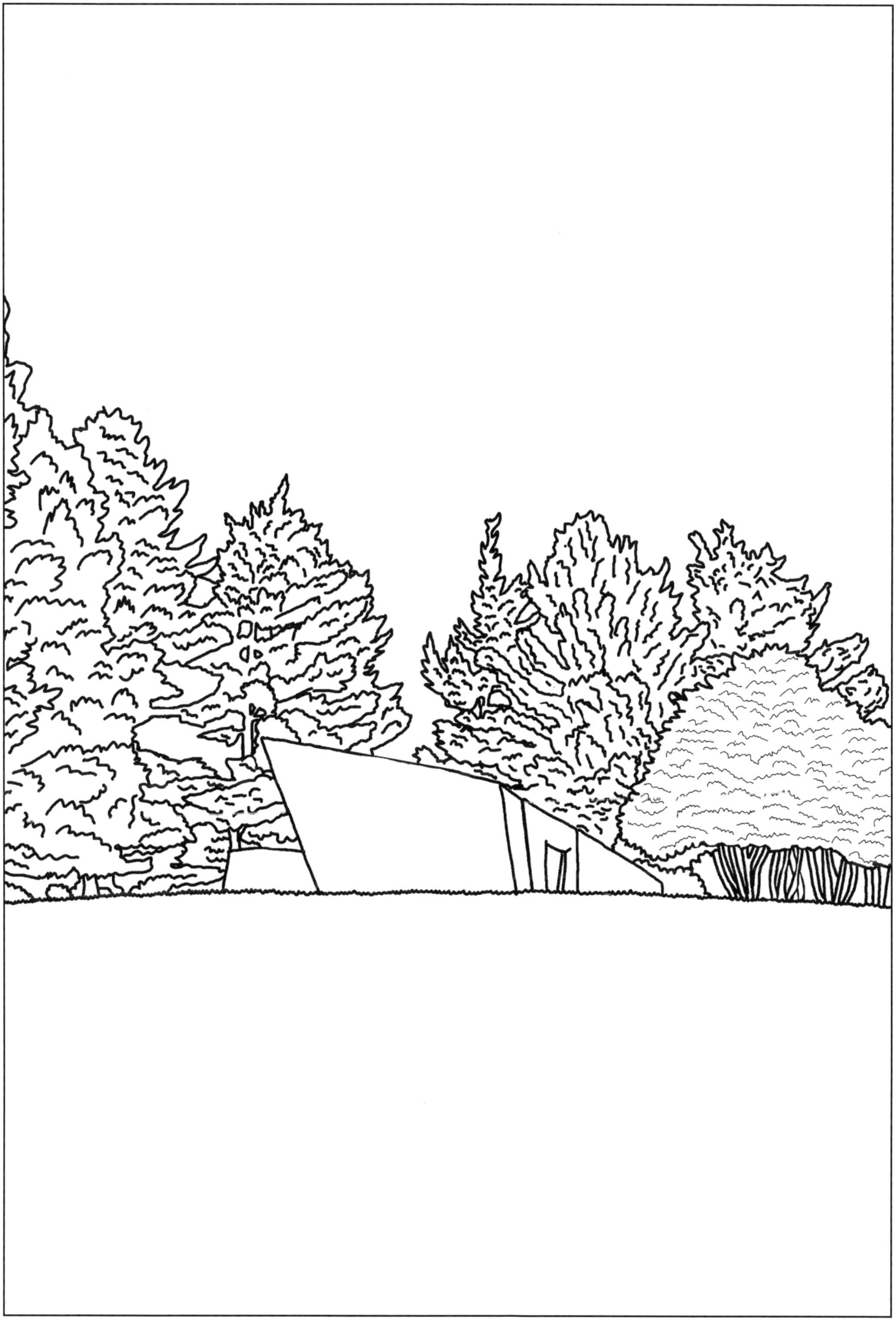

29. DA MONSTA

30. THE ENTRANCE TO DA MONSTA

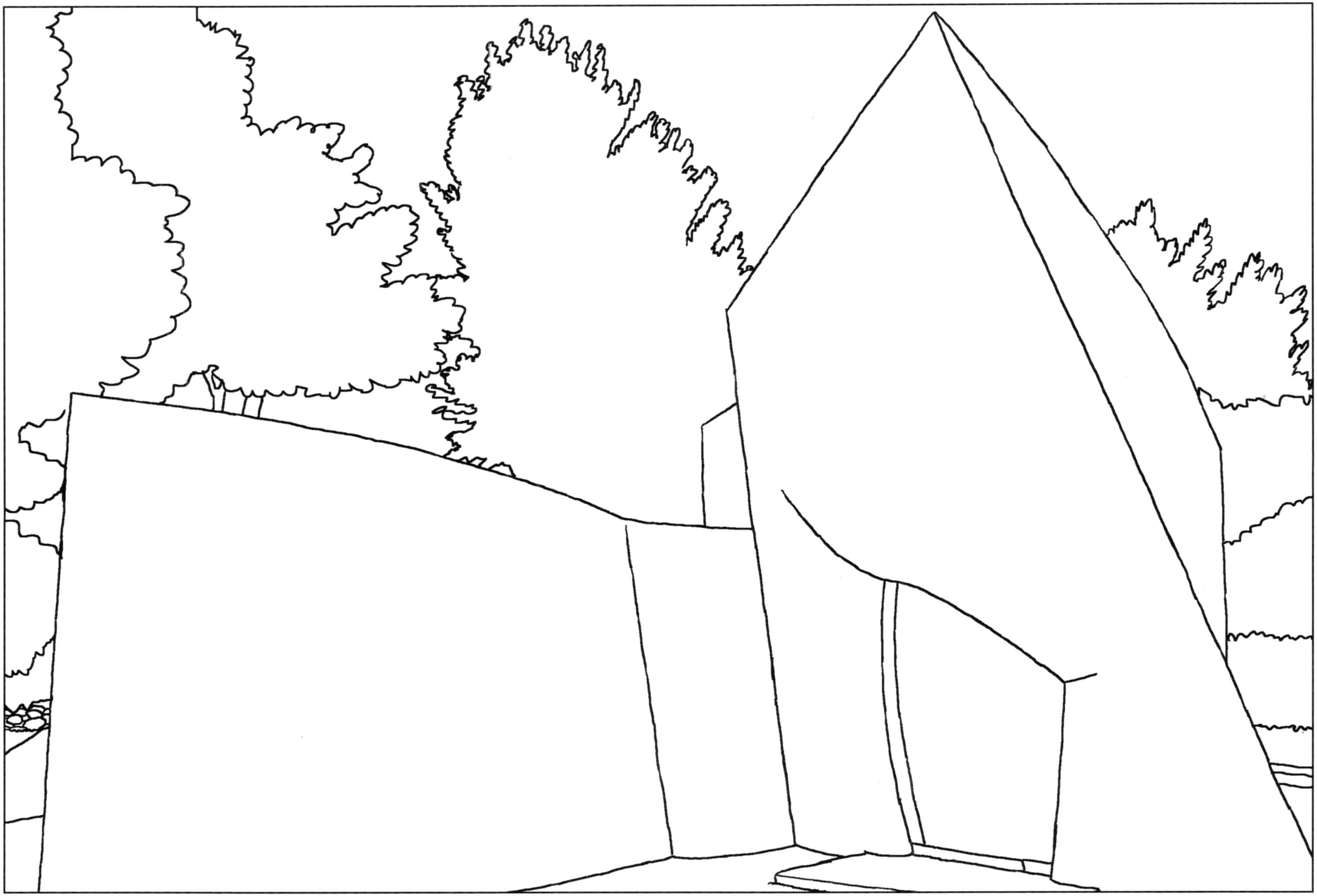

31. EXTERIOR OF DA MONSTA

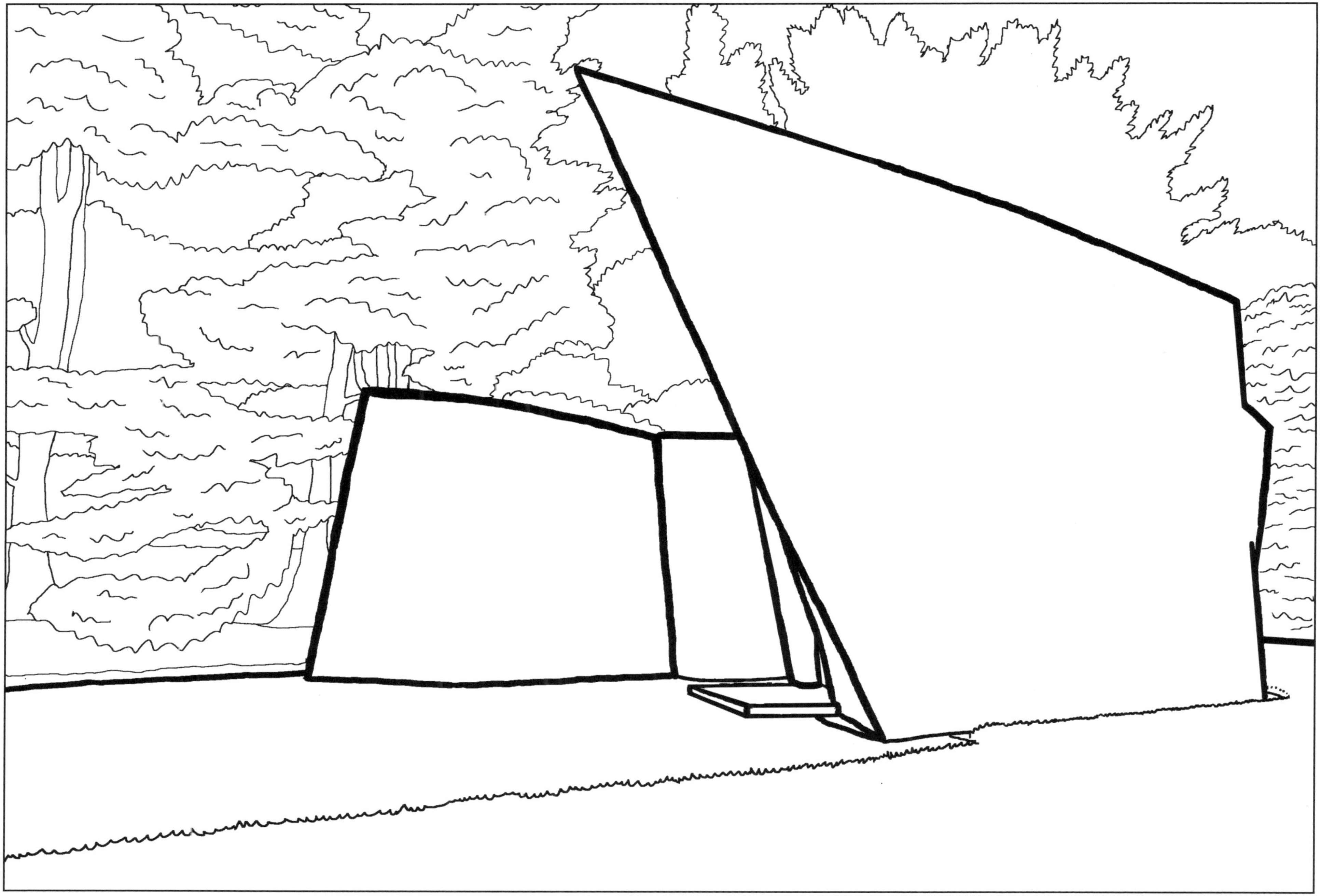

32. THE DOGHOUSE

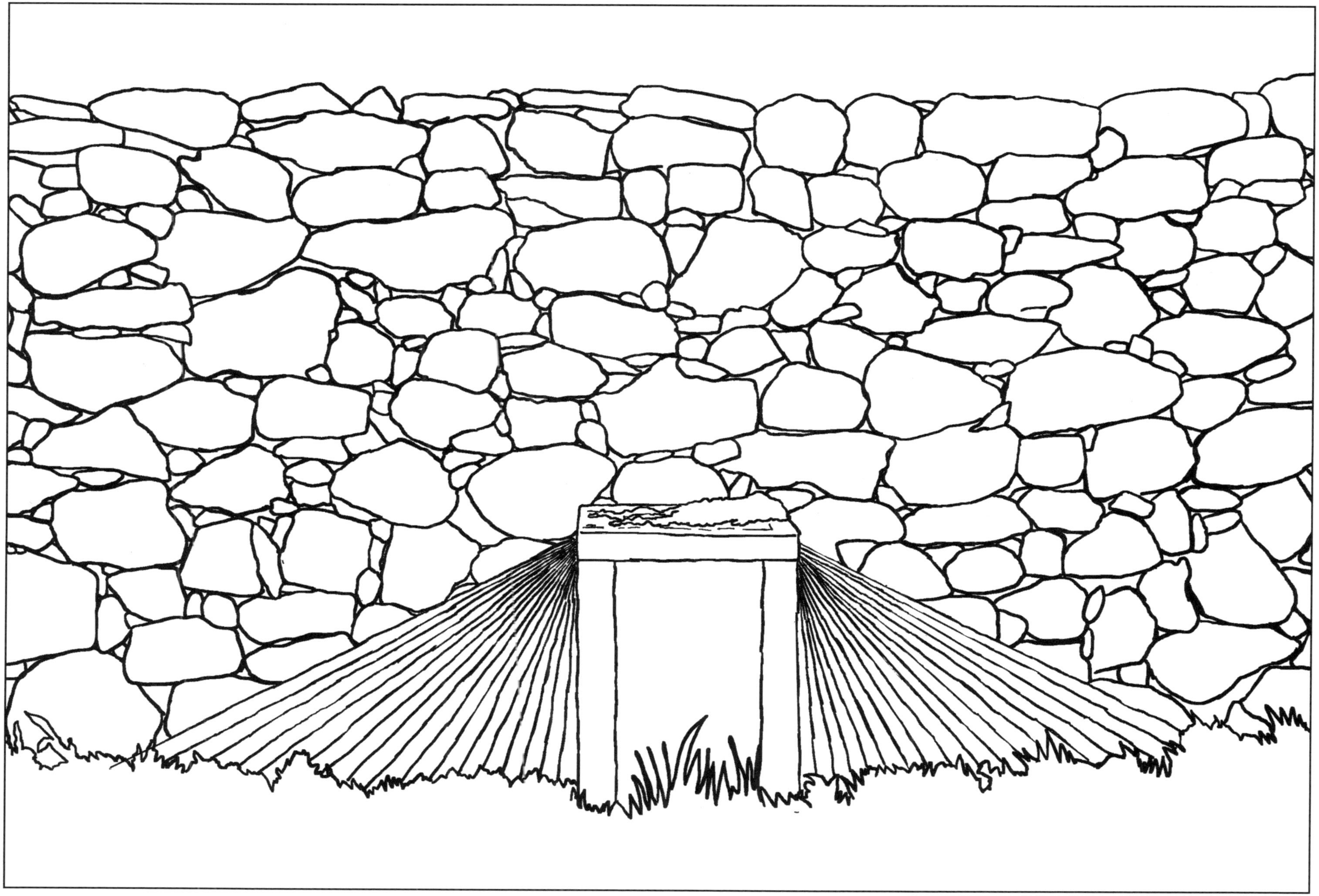

33. A LUTYENS-STYLE BENCH NEAR THE MONUMENT TO LINCOLN KIRSTEIN

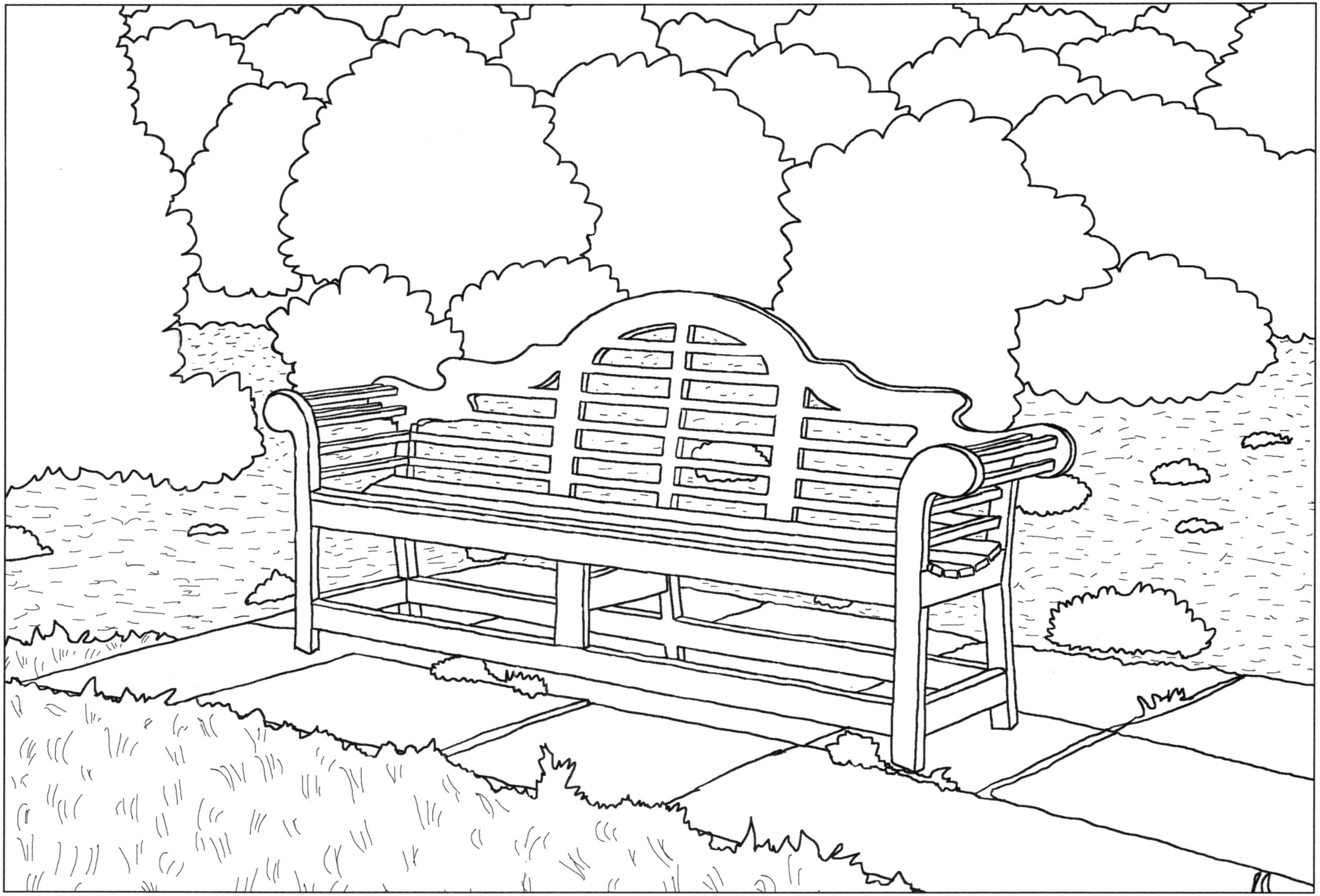

34. THE SUCCULENT GARDEN

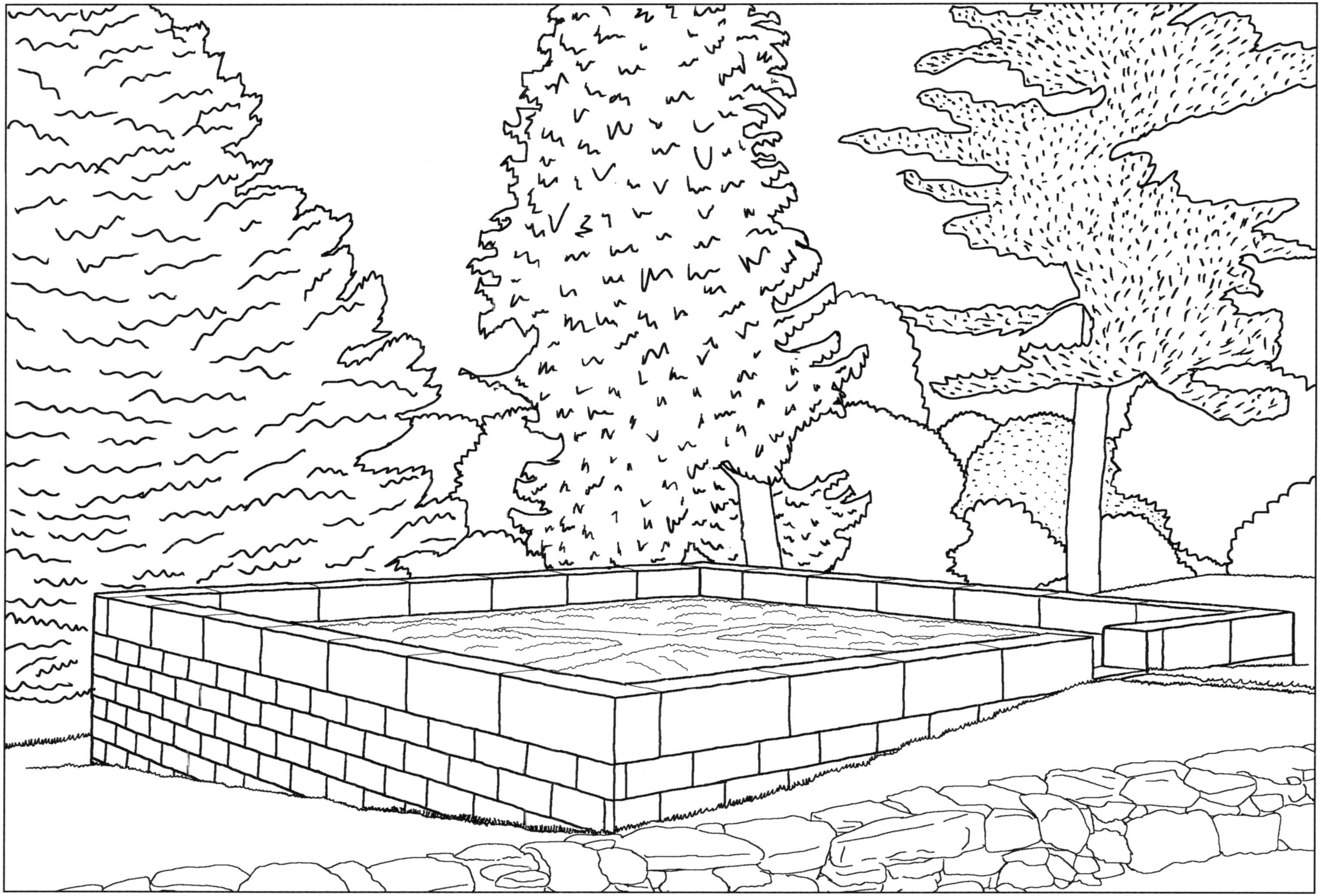

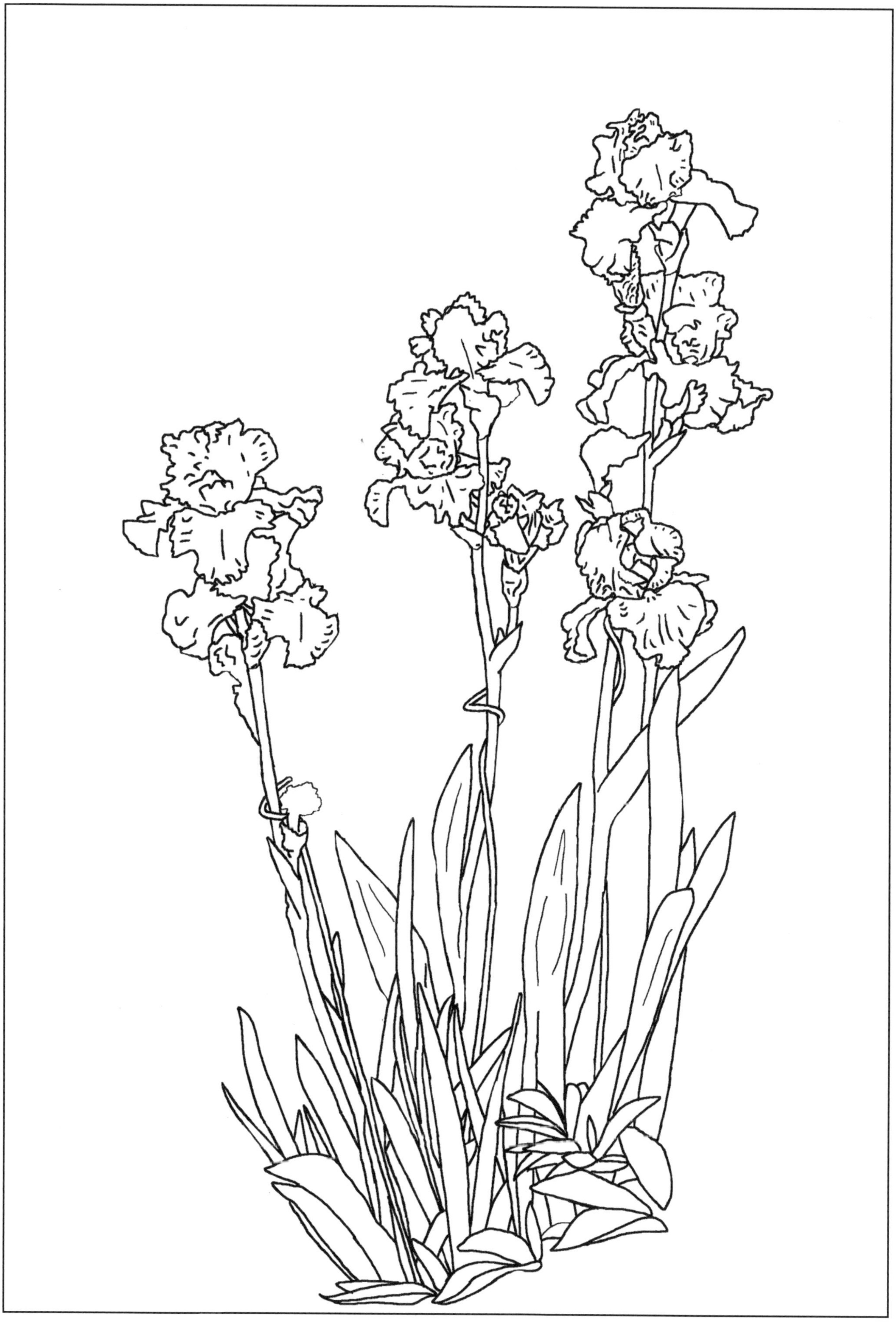

35. IRISES IN THE PEONY AND IRIS GARDEN

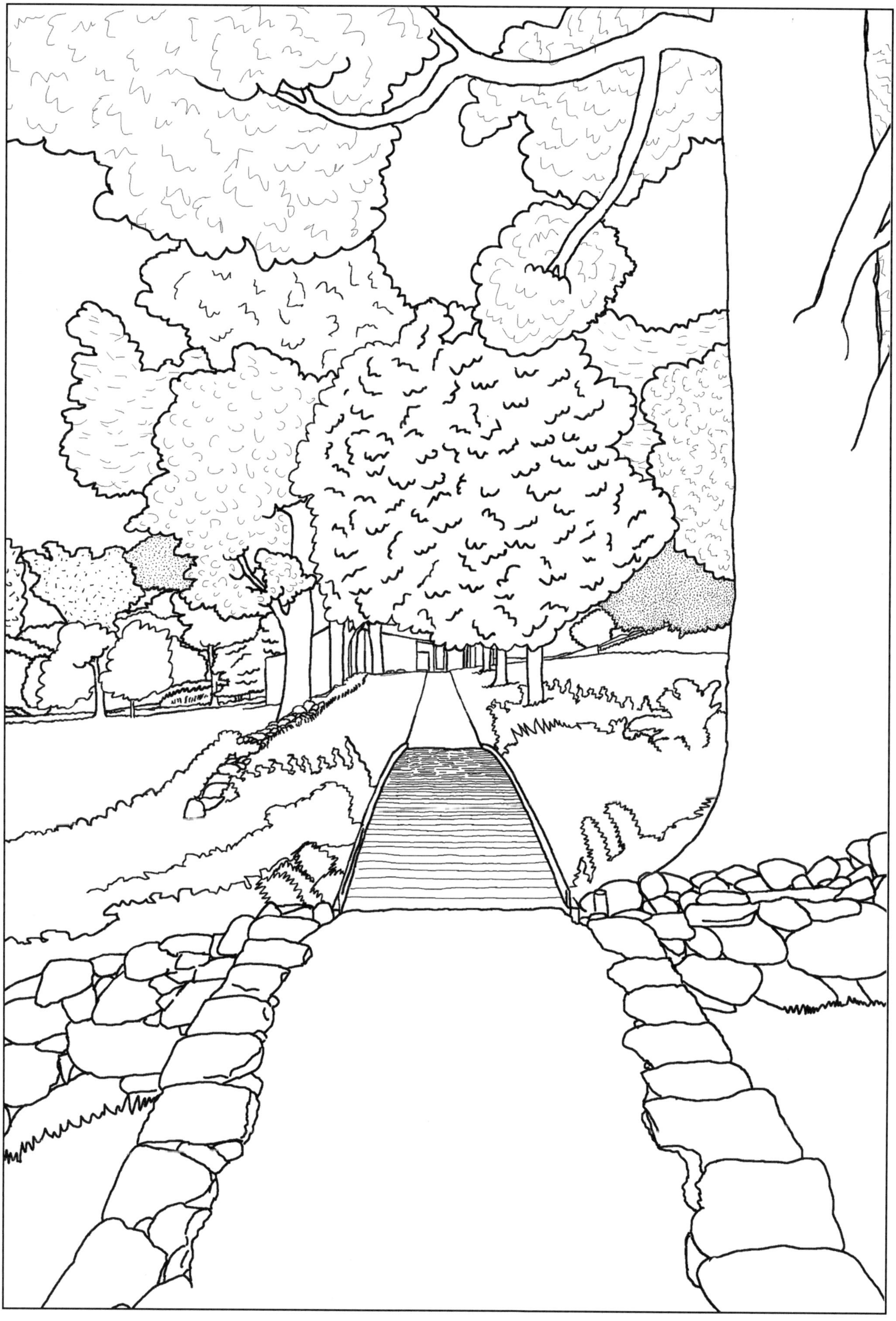

36. A WALKWAY THROUGH THE LANDSCAPE

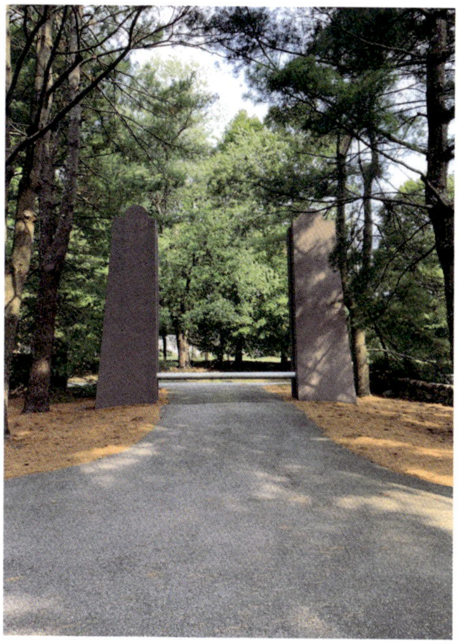

1. The Entrance Gate to the driveway, which dates from 1977, is flanked by two 20-foot-tall concrete pillars connected by an aluminum bar. Controlled by an electronic pulley system, the gate rises to admit guests and lowers to enclose the property.

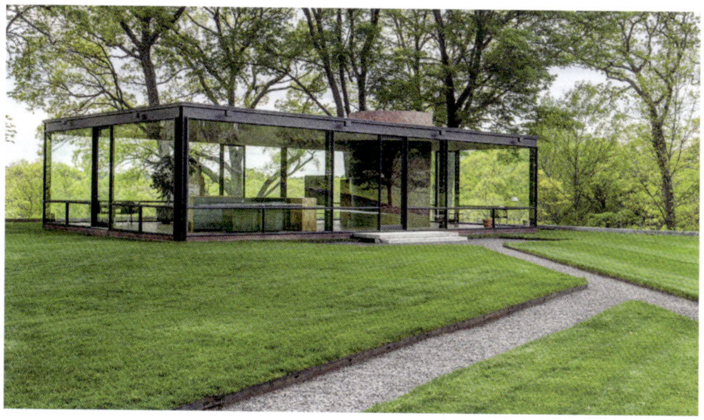

2. The Glass House is 55 feet long, 33 feet wide, and has 1,815 square feet of living space. The building helped usher in the International Style and is iconic because of its innovative use of materials and the way it blends into the landscape.

3. The Glass House as it is seen from the adjacent meadow shows the existing vernacular 18th- and 19th-century stone walls that were the "organizing principle" of the site.

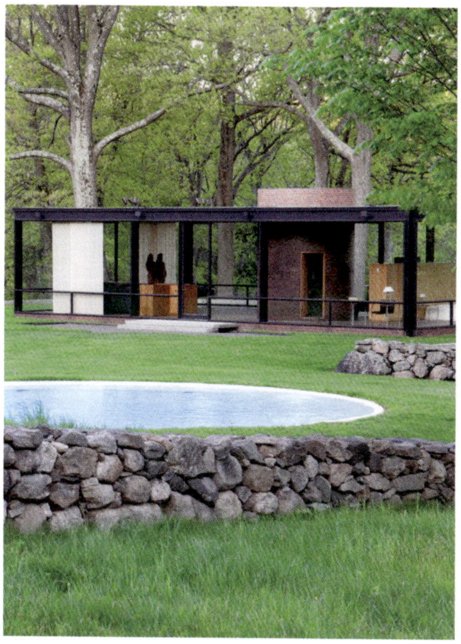

4. An exterior detail of the 1949 Glass House is best understood as a pavilion for viewing the surrounding landscape. Philip Johnson is famously quoted as saying, "I have very expensive wallpaper."

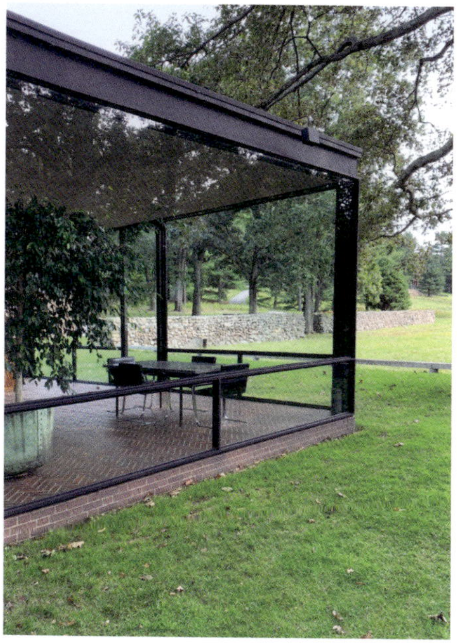

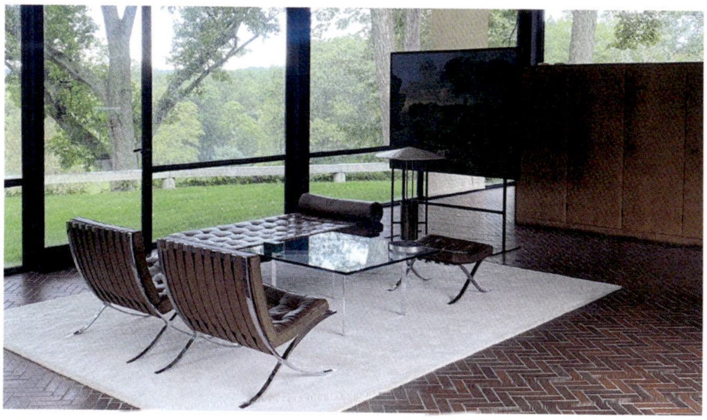

5. Since its completion, the building and its decor have not strayed from their original design. Most of the furniture came from Johnson's New York apartment, which was designed in 1930 by Ludwig Mies van der Rohe. Although there are no walls, Johnson referred to areas within the house as "rooms." A rug defines the living room area, while seating around a low table anchors the space. The living room is the focal point of the house.

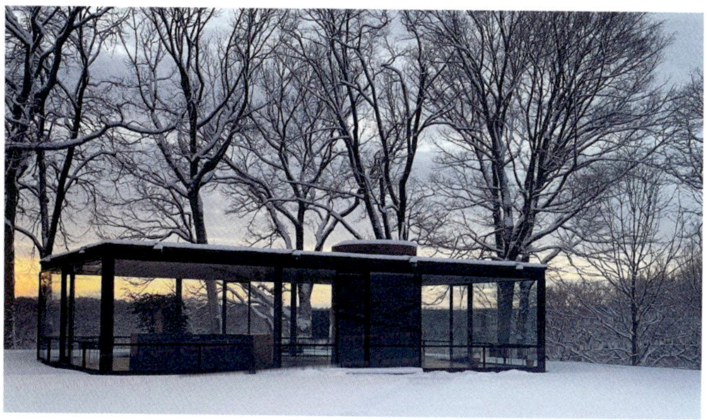

6. The "wallpaper" of the Glass House changes with the seasons. Oriented on the edge of the promontory, the sunsets viewed from the house are spectacular.

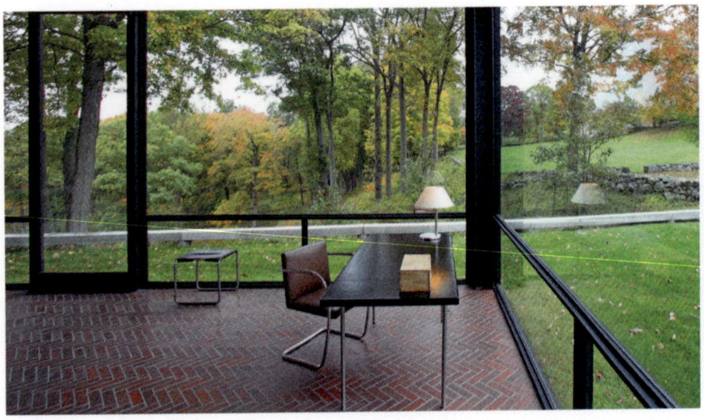

7. Delineated by a Mies van der Rohe leather and tubular steel stool, a small study space adjoins the bedroom. The study looks out onto the lawn and consists of a leather writing table by Mies van der Rohe and one of the architect's Brno tubular chairs, a Walter von Nessen Swing-arm table lamp, and a 19th-century American tiger maple box.

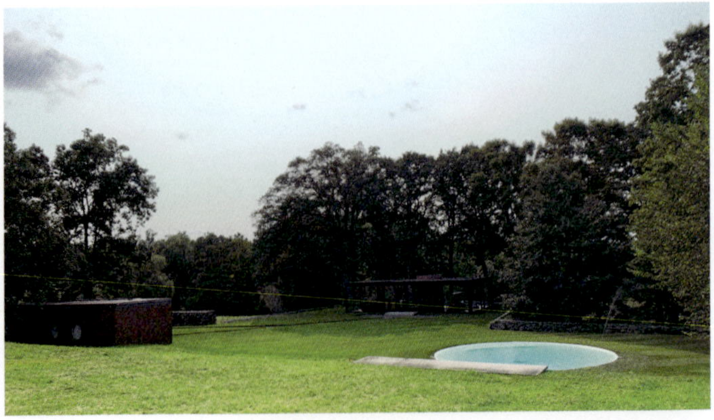

8. The Glass House Lawn is composed of the Glass House, the Brick House, and the 1955 pool. The repetition of rectangular and circular shapes creates a serene order, directing the eye throughout the landscape.

9. Comprised of a handmade double bed, Mies van der Rohe's glass and tubular steel table, and Wilhelm Wagenfeld and Carl Jakob Jucker's Bauhaus lamp, the bedroom is pared down to the essential items. Pillows were stored in the surrounding cupboards until they were needed.

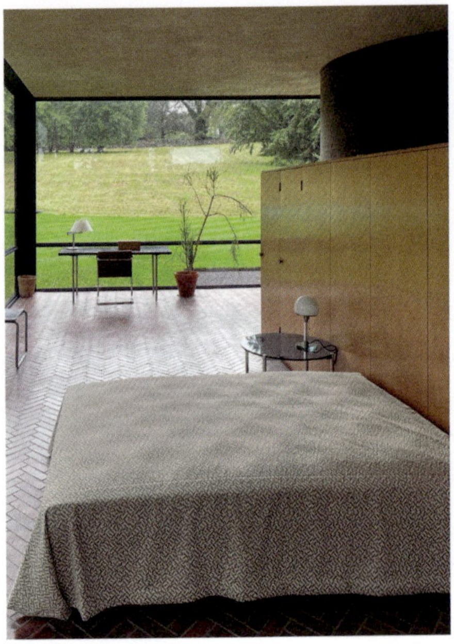

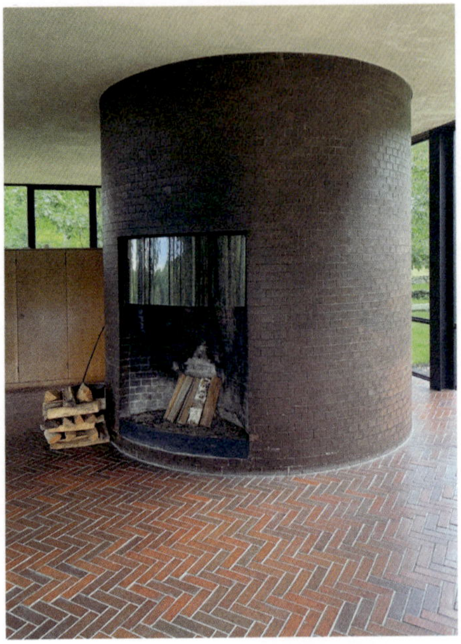

10. Enclosed within a brick cylinder, the fireplace in the Glass House is located on the other side of the bathroom. The strategic placement of these elements provides convenient and necessary ventilation. The cylinder provides an anchor from which the other planes radiate.

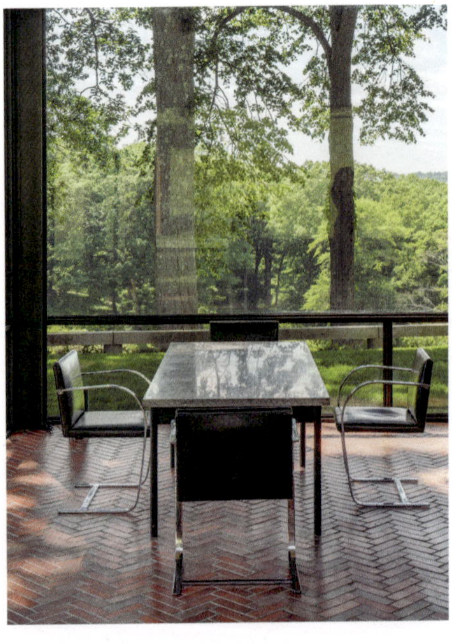

11. The dining table in the Glass House was designed by Johnson and is surrounded with Mies van der Rohe's Brno flat bar chairs, which date from 1929.

12. Each of the four walls of the Glass House is punctuated by a centrally located glass door that opens onto the landscape.

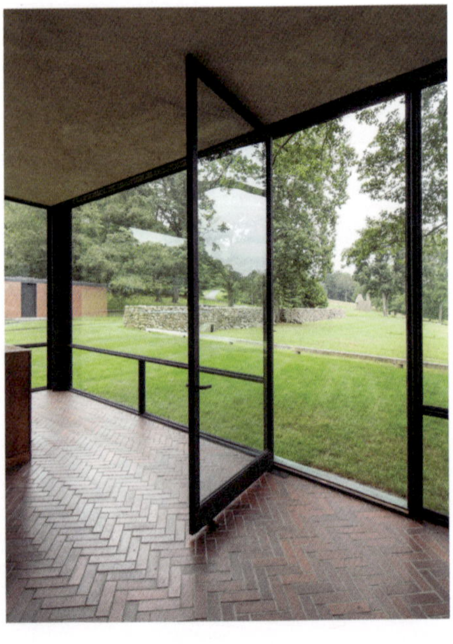

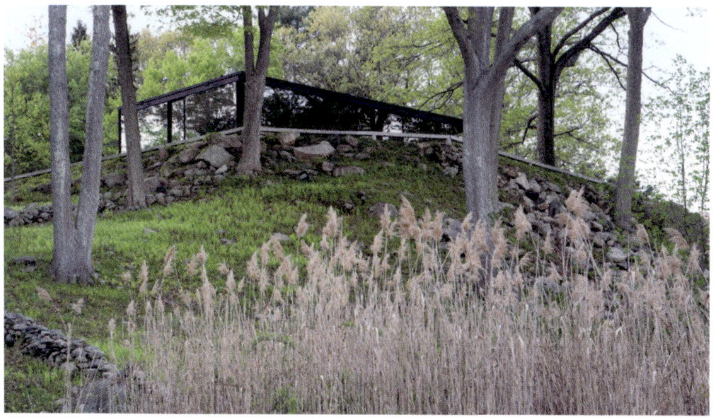

13. Invisible from the road, the Glass House sits on a wooded promontory overlooking a small pond and the surrounding woods.

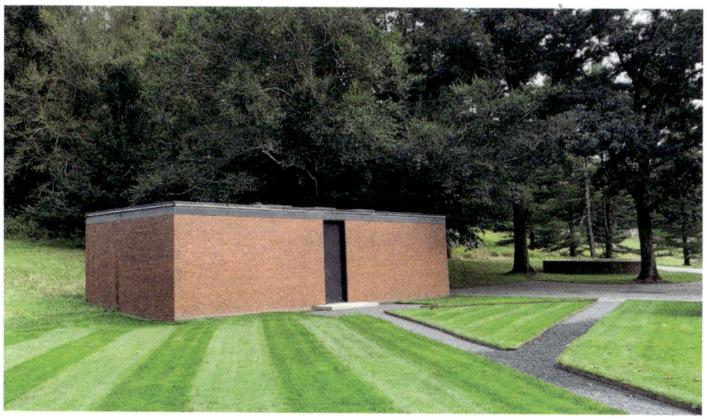

14. Designed and completed as part of the original composition of the site in 1949, the Brick House serves as a counterpoint to the transparency of the Glass House. Often serving as a guest house, the Brick House includes a bedroom, a library, a full bath, and the utilities needed for the pool and Glass House.

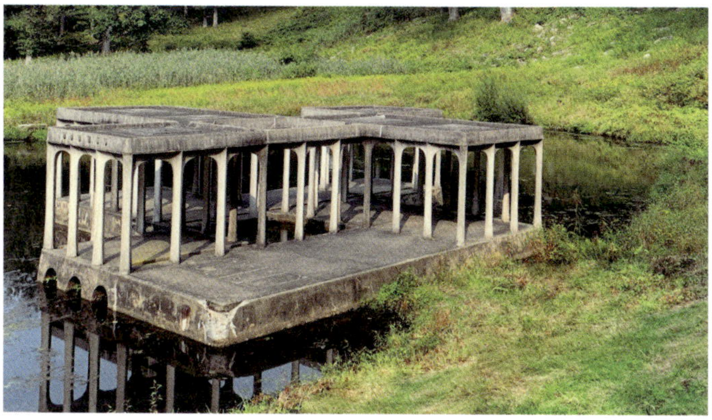

15. Pavilion in the Pond, 1962, is constructed of prefabricated concrete arches and poured concrete and sits in a man-made pond located at the bottom of a hill below the Glass House. The Pavilion is intentionally scaled down in size by one third, making it seem farther away than it actually is

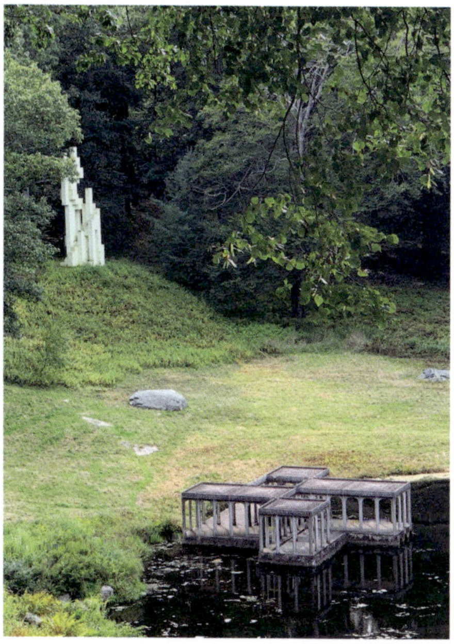

16. In the tradition of architectural follies in garden design, the Pavilion's scaled down size plays with the viewer's sense of perspective.

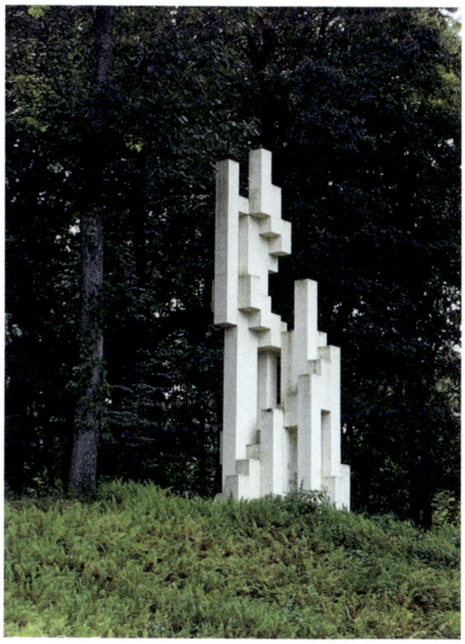

17. Johnson named this 1985 structure as a monument to his close friend, choreographer Lincoln Kirstein. The tower is 30 feet high and was intended to be climbed. Johnson described it as "a staircase to nowhere." The architect based the design partly on the geometry of dominoes and the choreography of George Balanchine.

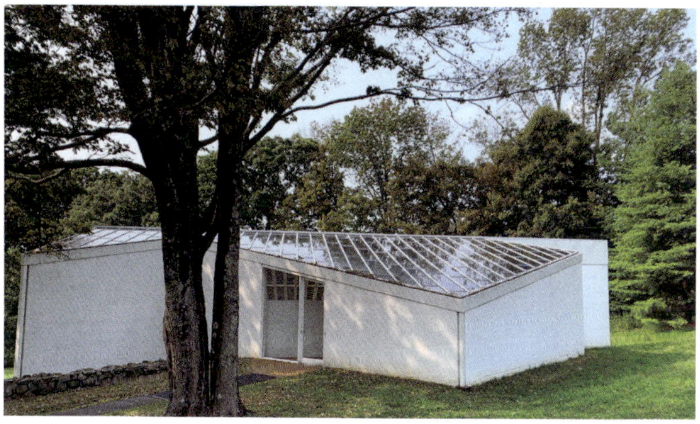

18. The Sculpture Gallery, 1970, is enclosed by a white brick and tubular steel skeleton which supports the building's aluminum and glass skylight.

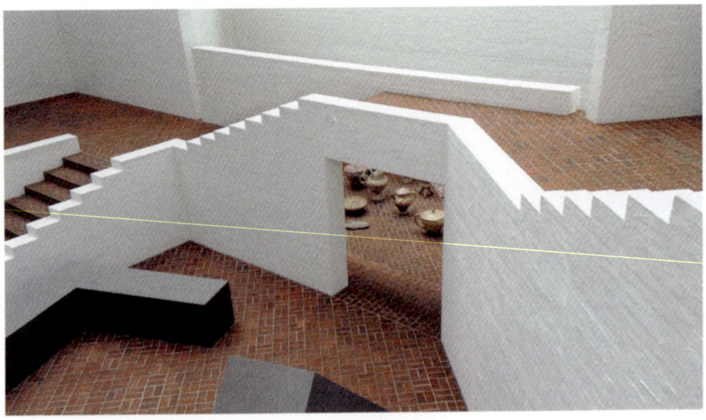

19. The Greek islands and their many villages were the inspiration for the Sculpture Gallery. The building's plan is made up of a series of squares set at 45-degree angles to each other and staircases that spiral down past a series of bays that display sculpture.

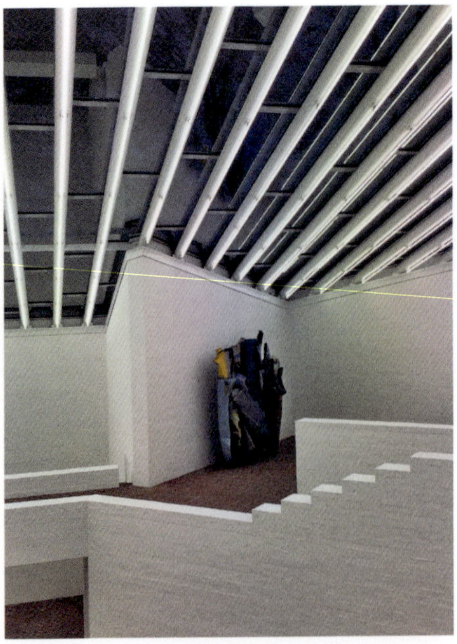

20. The inside of the Sculpture Gallery is illuminated by a cold cathode lighting system which is suspended from a steel support system. The sculpture is John Chamberlain's *The Archbishop, The Golfer, and Ralph*, 1982–1983.

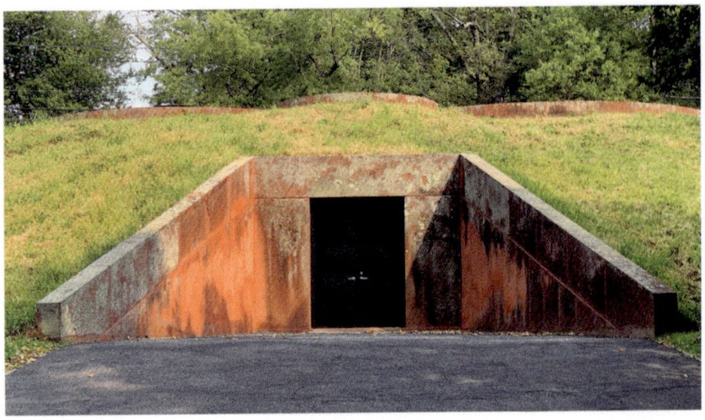

21. Johnson designed the Painting Gallery, 1965, to house the collection of large-scale modern paintings that he and his partner, David Whitney, collected throughout their lives. The exterior of the gallery is a grass-covered mound, topped by a low parapet with a monumental stone entrance inspired by the Greek Treasury of Atreus from 1250 BCE, flanked by red sandstone.

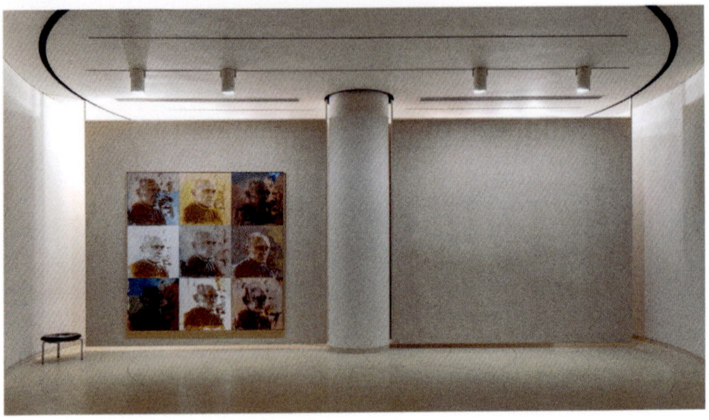

22. An exterior parapet traces the Painting Gallery's interior plan of three circles in various diameters. In each of the circular rooms, a rotating rack for artworks displays one or two paintings per manually operated spindle. Although Johnson preferred to view six works at a given time, this device allowed for the storage of up to 42 paintings. Above is *Philip Johnson*, 1972, by Andy Warhol.

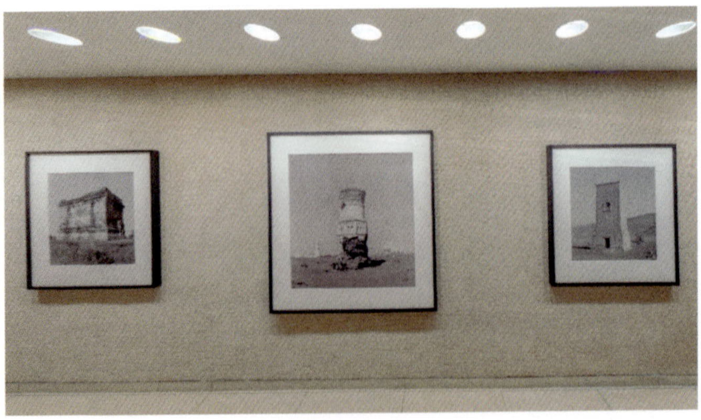

23. Hanging in the vestibule of the Painting Gallery are works by Lynn Davis from her *Monument* series. *From left: Library, Pagan, Burma, 1993*; *Minaret, Port of Mokka, Yemen, 1996*; *Tomb Palmyra, Syria, 1995.* The placement of Davis' work pays homage to Johnson's inspiration for the exterior of the building, the Treasury of Atreus, an ancient Greek tomb.

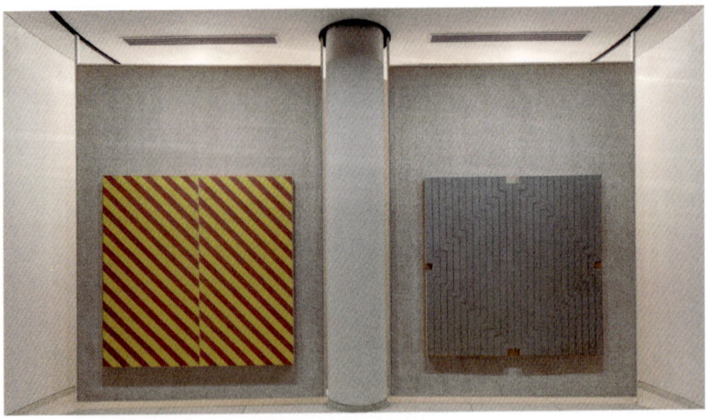

24. Johnson and Whitney were early admirers of Frank Stella, and they avidly collected the artist's work throughout their lives. The Glass House contains a significant collection of works by Stella, which range from painting to sculpture to multimedia. Frank Stella's *Tetuan II,* 1964, *left*, and *Averroes,* 1960, are shown above.

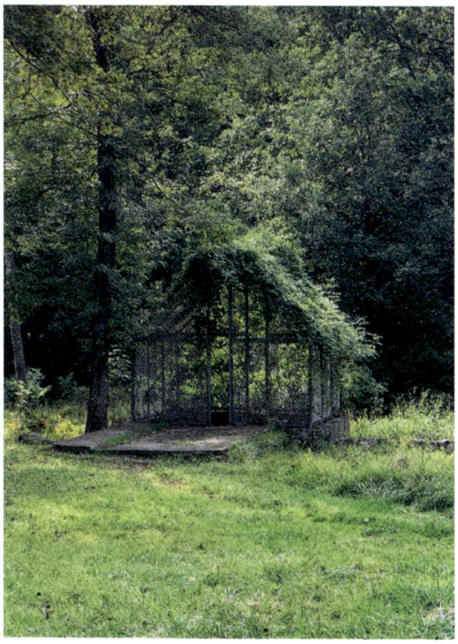

25. The chain link material, from which the Ghost House, 1984, was constructed, provides no shelter from the elements, but its form references that of a traditional home.

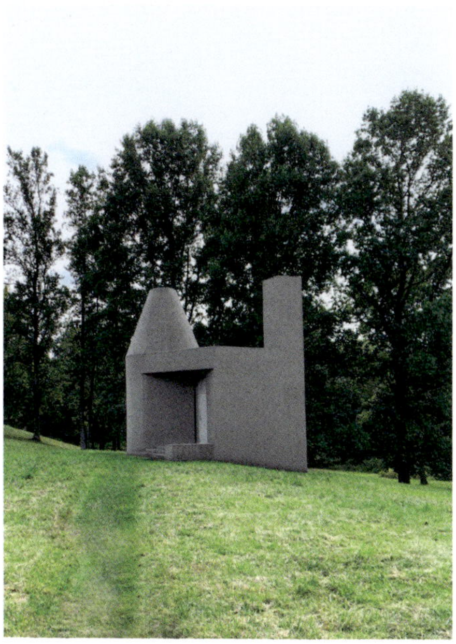

26. The Studio, 1980, a one-room workspace and architecture library, is approached through a field of tall grass and wetlands.

27. The interior walls of the Studio are lined with bookcases filled with 1,400 volumes on architecture.

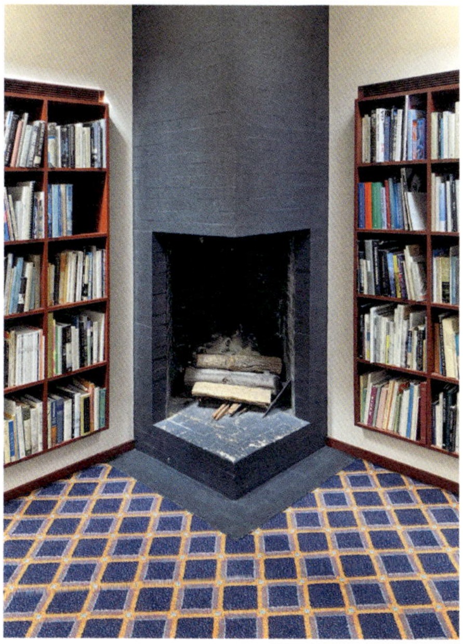

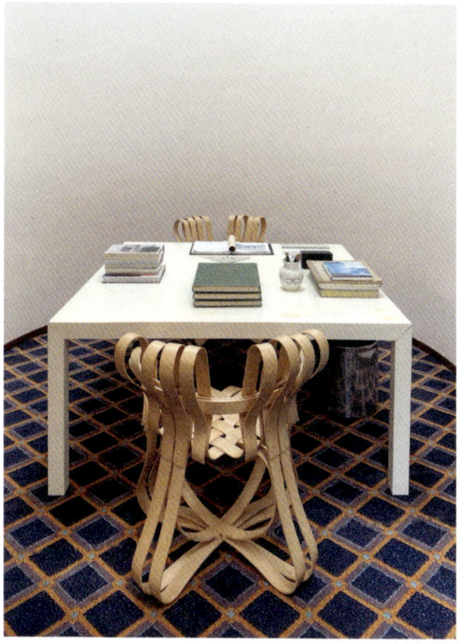

28. The Studio provides a peaceful place to work, surrounded by what Johnson called "the most exciting decoration in the world." Two bentwood Cross Check armchairs by Frank Gehry for Knoll provide seating.

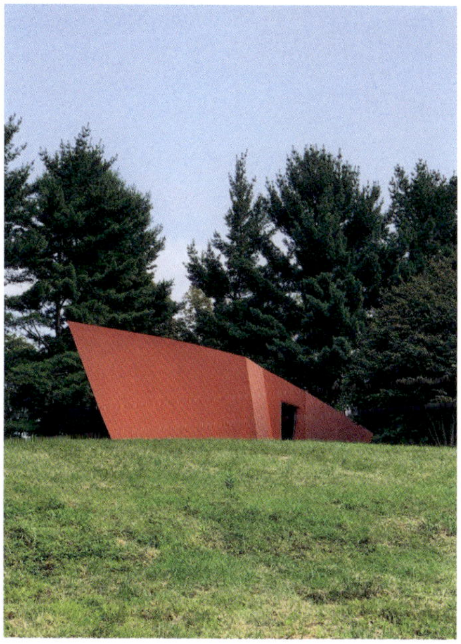

29. Johnson claimed that his original inspiration for Da Monsta, 1995, came from the design for a museum in Dresden by Frank Stella.

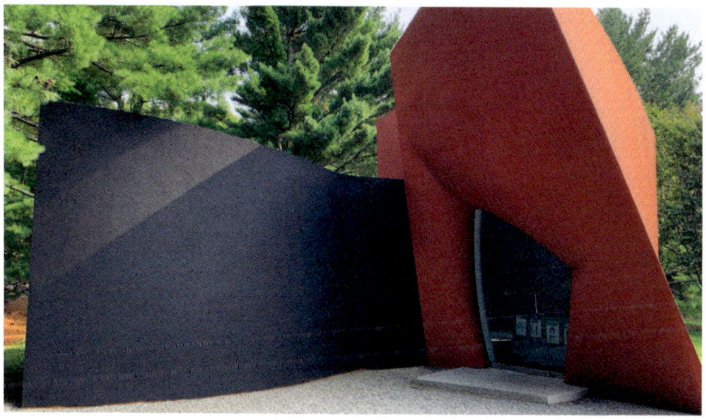

30. Da Monsta, constructed of modified gunite, uses warped and torqued forms. The name of the building is an adaptation of "monster." Johnson felt the building had the quality of a living thing.

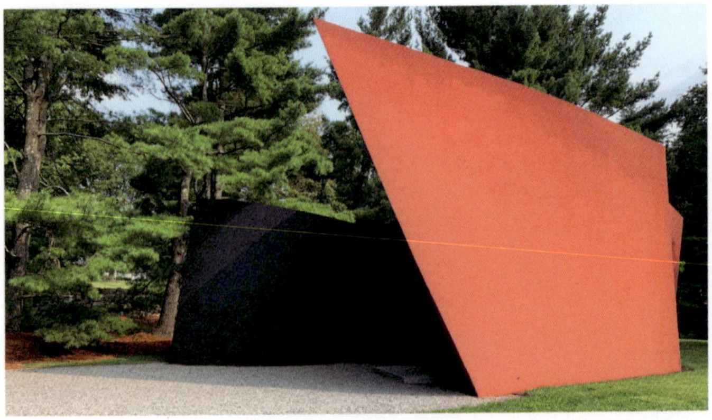

31. Located near the entrance gate, Da Monsta is a jagged neo-Expressionist building of curves and contours painted in custom hues of red and black.

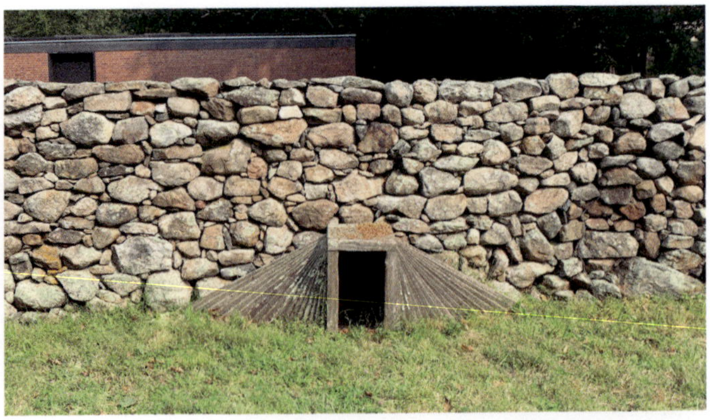

32. The small doghouse was created by Johnson in 1997 as a conceptual project for a classically inspired tomb. However, when completed, the small wooden object turned out to be just the right size for his and Whitney's new puppies, hence the nickname for the structure, "Doghouse."

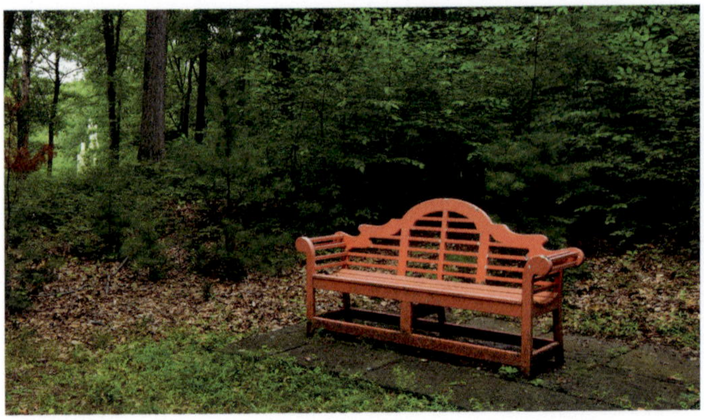

33. A Lutyens-style bench, from about 1998, stands in a clearing beyond the Monument to Lincoln Kirstein.

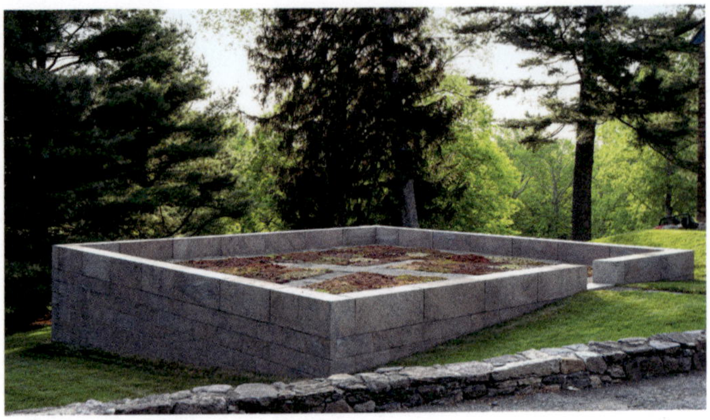

34. Calluna, named for the scientific genus for common heather, was Whitney's home. In 1989, he designed a succulent garden in the front yard of Calluna that was influenced by Kazimir Malevich's *Suprematist Composition* of 1916, a drawing Whitney acquired in 1989. The base of the garden was constructed with the same pink granite as that used in Johnson's AT&T Building, 1984.

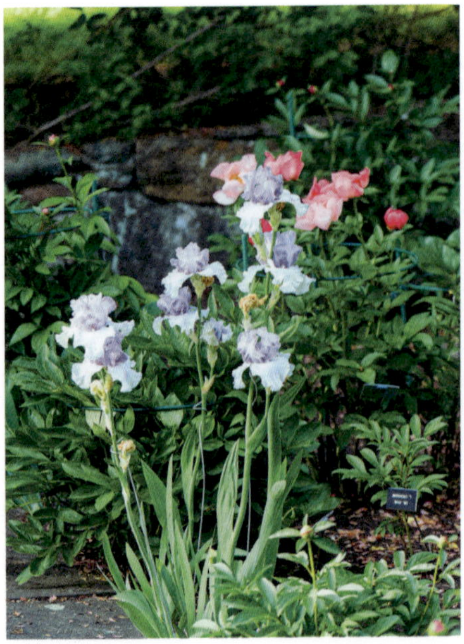

35. Whitney was an avid gardener and established a spectacular garden at Grainger, the circa-1783 home he purchased in 1990. The garden includes peonies and irises. During his lifetime, Whitney was the only person permitted to work in the peony and succulent gardens.

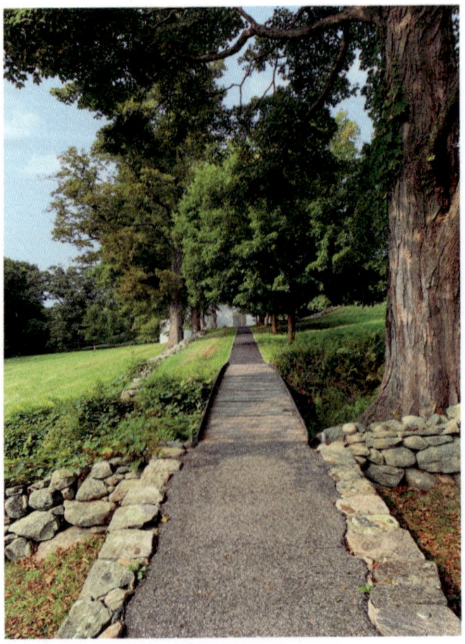

36. Johnson purchased the initial five-acre parcel in late 1945. Consecutive land purchases over the years brought the site up to its current 49 acres, creating a canvas for 14 architectural structures.

VIK MUNIZ was born in São Paulo, Brazil, in 1961, and now lives and works in New York. Muniz creates meticulously crafted visual puns and games, delighting viewers while at the same time raising more thoughtful questions about the nature and mechanics of illusion and representation. Muniz draws with unusual materials, such as chocolate, ash, dirt, or bits of paper, creating *trompe l'oeil* renderings (often of iconic artworks and culturally resonant imagery), which he later photographs into his own, final artwork. His highly constructed works are not only readable on various levels but also call attention to their own legibility, conveying an image without concealing the language—or rather, the linguistics—of the image conveyed. Muniz has had numerous solo museum exhibitions—including at the Art Museum of Banco de la República, Bogotá (2013), the Beyeler Foundation (2012), P.S.1 MoMA (2007), the Baltic Centre for Contemporary Art (2007), the Pinacoteca do Estado de São Paulo (2004), MACRO (2004), the Irish Museum of Modern Art (2004), and the Menil Collection (2002).

DAVID WALLACE CROTTY was born in Cohasset, Massachusetts, and grew up in Freeport, Maine. Crotty began drawing as a toddler, eventually winning The Portland Maine Sunday Telegram Annual Christmas Art Contest when he was just six years old. While in high school, he took advanced drawing classes at the Portland School of Art. After high school he moved to New Haven, Connecticut, where he regularly contributed illustrations to the *Yale Daily News*. In 1983, he moved to New York and attended the NYU Tisch School of the Arts, where he studied film production, animation, and film history. After graduating, Crotty worked in television commercial production, continuing to draw and paint, and adding film and photography to his artistic expression. Crotty's first coloring book, created in 2007, was a three-volume set of books for the Maysles Films documentary, *Grey Gardens*. Subsequent coloring books include *Landmarks of Hollywood*, *The Palm Springs Coloring Books*, and *The Hearst Castle Coloring Book*.

PAUL GOLDBERGER, whom the *Huffington Post* has called "the leading figure in architecture criticism," is a contributing editor at *Vanity Fair*. He is the former architecture critic of both *The New Yorker* and the *New York Times*, where his architecture criticism was awarded the Pulitzer Prize, the highest award in journalism. He is the author of numerous books, including *DUMBO: The Making of a Neighborhood and the Rebirth of Brooklyn*; *BALLPARK: Baseball in the American City*; *Building Art: The Life and Work of Frank Gehry*; *Why Architecture Matters*; *Christo and Jeanne-Claude*, and *Building Up and Tearing Down*. He holds the Joseph Urban Chair in Design and Architecture at The New School in New York City, and was formerly dean of the Parsons School of Design. He is the chair of the Advisory Council of the Glass House and is a trustee emeritus of the National Trust for Historic Preservation.

SCOTT DREVNIG joined the Glass House in 2012 and has served as its deputy director since 2015. As an employee of The National Trust for Historic Preservation, he works to fundraise and preserve one of the world's most celebrated modernist works. Drevnig manages all development initiatives, institutional and individual giving, and special events nationwide for this renowned site, while creating significant corporate partnerships. Previously he worked as a director of art and event marketing and senior account manager within nonprofit/ marketing organizations such as Warner Communications and Christie's. He holds three advanced degrees including a Masters in Business Administration from New York University's Stern School of Business.

ACKNOWLEDGMENTS

The Glass House would like to thank Beth Rudin DeWoody, one of our inaugural Glass House Advisory Council members. It is her passion for art and design, and her keen insights that led her to suggest a coloring book, and we couldn't be more grateful.

Thank you to Vik Muniz for his beautiful cover. We also wish to thank our illustrator David Crotty, whose stunning drawings ensured this project could be realized. Thank you as well to Paul Goldberger for his generous contribution, the foreword to this book.

A very special thank you to Isabel Richards, Glass House development manager, for her essential assistance with project management, which guaranteed this book could make its deadlines. Gratitude and thanks go to Gregory Sages, executive director, and the entire Glass House team for helping make this project a reality.

Thank you also to the photographers Stacy Bass, Paul Bickford, Michael Biondo, Robin Hill, and Paul Warchol for their beautiful images of the Glass House and its site. At Pointed Leaf Press, special thanks go to Suzanne Slesin, publisher, and Frederico Farina, creative director.

Additional recognition and thanks to the members of the Glass House Advisory Council: Barry Bergdoll, Beth Rudin DeWoody, Susan Magrino Dunning, Paul Goldberger (chair), Edwin B. Hathaway, Anthony Ingrao, Reed Krakoff, Martha Nelson, Jeffrey R. Peltier, Margaret Russell, Pamela Sanders, William Sofield, Robert A. M. Stern, Mimi Reichert Sternlicht, Kay Unger, Rose Uniacke, and Edwina von Gal.
—**Scott Drevnig**, Deputy Director, October 2021

PHOTOGRAPHY CREDITS

All photographs Courtesy of the Glass House with the exception of the following:
Stacy Bass: Inside front cover and page 1; page 89, *center row, left*; page 91, *top row, left.*
Paul Bickford: page 94, *center row, right*; and *bottom row, left.*
Michael Biondo: page 5; pages 8–9; pages 10–11, pages 12–13, pages 14–15; page 89, *top row, right*; page 92, *center row, right*; and *bottom row, right*; inside back cover.
Robin Hill: pages 6–7; page 90, *top row, left*; and *bottom row, right*; page 94, *center row, left.*
Paul Warchol: page 2.

CREDITS FOR THE WORKS OF ART

Page 2, *Untitled*, 1965–1970, by Robert Morris © 2021 The Estate of Robert Morris / Artists Rights Society (ARS), New York.
Page 92, *top row, right*: *The Archbishop, The Golfer, and Ralph*, 1982–1983, by John Chamberlain © 2021 Fairweather & Fairweather LTD / Artists Rights Society (ARS), New York.
Page 92, *center row, right*: *Philip Johnson,* 1972, by Andy Warhol © 2021 The Andy Warhol Foundation for the Visual Arts, Inc. / Licensed by Artists Rights Society (ARS), New York.
Page 92, *bottom row, right*: *Tetuan II,* 1964; and *Averroes*, 1960, by Frank Stella © 2021 Frank Stella / Artists Rights Society (ARS), New York.

CAPTIONS

COVER Artwork by Vik Muniz.
INSIDE COVER AND PAGE 1 The Glass House at dawn.
OPPOSITE TITLE PAGE The Sculpture Gallery interior with shadows.
PAGE 5 Exterior detail of the Glass House.
PAGES 6–7 The Glass House at sunset.
PAGES 8–9 Pavilion in the Pond with a cloudy sky.
PAGES 10–11 The Brick House with the Studio in the background.
PAGES 12–13 A view of the Studio with the Glass House in the distance. Johnson often referred to himself as a landscape architect and when asked to compare architecture and landscape, he stated, "to me, it's one art."
PAGES 14–15 The Ghost House.
OPPOSITE The Glass House.

THE GLASS HOUSE

199 Elm Street, New Canaan, CT 06840
203 594 9884
theglasshouse.org
Follow us:
INSTAGRAM: @theglasshouse_newcanaan
FACEBOOK: @PJGlassHouse
TWITTER: @PJGlassHouse

The Glass House, built between 1949 and 1995 by architect Philip Johnson (1906–2005), is a site of the National Trust for Historic Preservation located in New Canaan, Connecticut. The pastoral 49-acre landscape comprises 14 structures, including the Glass House,1949, and features a permanent collection of 20th-century American painting and sculpture, along with temporary exhibitions.
Tours of the site are available from April through December and advance reservations are required. Private tours are available year-round.
The Glass House serves as a catalyst for the preservation and interpretation of modern architecture, art, design, and landscape.

PUBLISHER/EDITORIAL DIRECTOR Suzanne Slesin
CREATIVE DIRECTOR Frederico Farina

ISBN: 978-0-9777875-7-9
First Edition 10 9 8 7 6 5 4 3 2 1
Printed in Spain

POINTED LEAF PRESS, LLC, 136 Baxter Street, Suite 1C, New York, NY 10013.